Moving
Mountains

Moving Mountains

John Waters

TRIANGLE

First published in Great Britain in 1999
Society for Promoting Christian Knowledge
Holy Trinity Church
Marylebone Road
London NW1 4DU

British Library Cataloguing-in-Publication Data

A catalogue record of this book is available from the British Library

ISBN 0–281–05098–8

Bible quotations are from the *Contemporary English Version*
unless otherwise stated.
Quotations from the *Contemporary English Version* (CEV) are
Copyright © American Bible Society, 1995.
Quotations marked *RSV* are from the *Revised Standard Version*
of the Bible © 1971 and 1952.
Those marked *NIV* are from the *New International Version*,
copyright © 1973, 1978, 1984 by the International Bible Society,
published by Hodder & Stoughton.

Typeset in Sabon by
Pioneer Associates, Perthshire
Printed in Great Britain by
Caledonian International, Glasgow

CONTENTS

CHRONOLOGY

979   27 November: miracle of the moving of
Muqattam Mountain through the prayers
of Simaan the Tanner.

1890s   Migrations of Muslim people from oases to Cairo.

1900s   Migrations of poor Christian families from
Upper Egypt to Cairo and their engagement in
rubbish collection.

1969   Government moves the rubbish collectors to
Manshiyat Nasir district, under Muqattam
Mountain.

1972   The rubbish collector Qiddees invites Brother
Farahat to visit his people, the *zeballeen*.

1974   Brother Farahat comes to the *zeballeen* area.
First meeting of church in building of
corrugated iron. Bishop Samweel registers
Society of Rubbish Collectors.

1975   Brother Farahat's wife, Su'aad, starts a school
with two kindergarten classes.

1976   Fire destroys Manshiyat Nasir: redevelopment
begins. Construction of church below the
mountain on a site of 1,000 square metres.
Healing of Adham's head. First visit of the
Coptic Patriarch, Pope Shenouda.

1978   Ordination of Brother Farahat as Father Simaan.
First modern celebration of festival of St Simaan.

1980s	World Bank, Egyptian government and private agencies get involved in redeveloping Manshiyat Nasir. Rubbish collection service extended to low-income families.
1986	Opening of 'the cavern' as a permanent place of worship. Discovery of site of Anba Boula.
1991	Opening of the Church of Anba Boula seating 400 people.
1992	Earthquake leads to resettlement of people from other parts of Cairo on the Muqattam Mountain. Some remains of St Simaan are brought in procession to the church named after him. (Other remains go to the Church of St Mary and the Hanging Church in Old Cairo.)
1993	School sponsored by the Patmos Foundation of Finland opens.
1994	Opening of Patmos Hospital. Re-opening of 'the cavern' as a Roman-style amphitheatre on a site of 10,000 square metres. Three other churches open for worship: St Mark, the Angel & St John and Anba Abraam.
1996	Father Simaan receives the Robert Pierce Award for Christian Service, presented by World Vision.
1997	Some 120,000 people visit the Muqattam Mountain site during two weeks of Ramadan, the Muslim month of fasting.

Transferring experience from one culture to another is a delicate process. My sincere thanks go to friends in Egypt, who shared their insights, and those in England (starting with Naomi Starkey), who helped me to express them to the British reader.

Preface
DO YOU BELIEVE IN MIRACLES?

Miracles strike us in two contradictory ways. We are attracted by anything that lifts us out of our everyday ruts, and gives us a glimpse of heaven. Yet we feel extremely sceptical about anything that seems to make nonsense of our rational and scientific way of viewing the universe. When it comes to the Gospels, we are attracted to Jesus as a human being, but often find it hard to explain and accept his miracles.

This book concerns the lives of a group of rubbish collectors living near Cairo. Their story brings the miracles of the Gospels abruptly into the present. Yet they trace the origins of their thriving and colourful church back to the days when St Mark, the evangelist and Gospel writer, came to Egypt. But the coming of the Muslims to Egypt in the seventh century began the process by which the Christians of Egypt found themselves a minority. Even today they are denied opportunities for promotion and advancement that would help the disadvantaged among them to escape from the poverty trap.

As we approach the millennium, there are still many people in the world living in appalling conditions. What hope would *you* have if your house were filled with other people's stinking rubbish, if deprivation and disease stalked the land, and pigs lived in your backyard?

People in conditions like these are sometimes more open to the power of God than we in the affluent West are. The beauty of our green landscapes, best-kept villages and multi-purpose shopping malls blinds us to the reality of life for many throughout the world. Admittedly we have emotional problems, and medical ones too, but the raw struggle for survival in a polluted and impoverished place is completely foreign to our perceptions.

When you cannot afford a doctor, when you can't find food, where will you turn? Do you commit physical and spiritual suicide by resorting to drink, drugs and crime – or do you put your faith in God? This book tells the very remarkable story of how faith can genuinely move mountains, and what God can achieve through those who truly put their trust in him.

Profile of a rubbish collector

It was Easter Day and I was following in the wake of a lay-worker who worked among the *zeballeen*, or rubbish collectors, of Cairo. He was marching through the flies and filth, visiting as many people as he could in the community. The people live out on the edge of the city, under the shadow of the Muqattam Hills. Every day the men bring back the refuse of the metropolis in trucks and donkey carts to their streets and homes. The women then sift through it and salvage anything useful. They give the food scraps to the animals, so dogs and donkeys (sometimes a dead dog or a disabled donkey), goats and pigs mill around in the mud-and-manure alleyways. It was in this scene of squalor that my friend proclaimed to all he met, 'Yesua Qam!' ('Christ has risen!').

What did it mean to them? That's just what he asked one young pig-keeper who had turned to Christ only a month before. The man had married at the age of sixteen and lived with his wife in a small room. He had no papers as his birth certificate had been burnt up in a fire. This meant he also had no identity card. In Egypt everyone carries an ID card: it states not only your name and parentage, but also your religion. Rather in the way that people in Britain used to put down on their hospital forms 'C of E' (even if they were not active Anglicans at all), so in Egypt nearly all non-Muslims put 'Christian' on their card.

Legally everyone in Egypt has to have a religion. The vast majority of the 10 per cent of Egyptians who are 'Christian' rather than Muslim identify themselves with the ancient Coptic Orthodox Church, but this doesn't mean that they are necessarily keen Orthodox Christians, or know anything about Christ. Some indeed are very zealous, but the average local Coptic church is doing extremely well if it can attract 10 per cent of the Copts in the district to attend on a regular basis. In many villages there are no churches at all, and in many cities there are not enough, since it is difficult – some would say impossible – to get permission to build a new church. There are many parts of Egypt where there is no church available to teach the Copts, and many may know more about how Muslims pray than how they should worship as Christians.

The rubbish collectors' community we are concerned with here had up until 1974 been one such place: the people knew nothing about Christ, and if they wanted to pray they might bring newspapers and spread them out on the ground in imitation of Muslim prayer mats. Our young pig-keeper had been like this – a Copt in name only, growing up among people who until 1974 had had no one to teach them the Coptic Orthodox faith. As he had no papers, he had no legal rights – but he did get the chance to hear the gospel. Although he had no ID card, most of the rubbish collectors were presumed to be originally from Christian families. This was important, because in Egypt there are tight restrictions on any evangelistic activities of the Church, especially if it is suspected that Muslims might get to hear the gospel. But in the pig-keeper's case, the Church felt free to visit him – and all the more so *because* he was a pig-keeper.

When it comes to hearing the gospel, what is the advantage of looking after pigs? Simply this. In any other part of Cairo, if a Copt were to play a Christian cassette tape so that it could be heard in the street, he would get a visit from Muslim fundamentalists. Rubbish collectors, however, are generally spared their attentions, and this was why my friend could march through the streets shouting 'Jesus is risen!' without molestation. Why is this? It is partly due to the fact that the rubbish collectors keep pigs. Pigs in Islam are considered to be unclean, and those who look after them are popularly viewed as sub-human. So to avoid defiling themselves, keen Muslims would not contemplate going into a rubbish collector's shack – especially if he was also a pig-keeper.

This particular young man kept his pigs downstairs on the ground floor, so no Muslim would dream of entering his house. Previously he had lived in a shack, but by carefully selling off a couple of pigs per year, he had managed to build a shell of a house out of breeze blocks. There was no plaster and no glass in the windows, so dust and ash from burnt rubbish could freely blow in.

To make our visit more comfortable the pig-keeper put some pieces of cardboard across the gaping windows to stop the worst of the dirt from blowing in. We sat at a table – the one prominent piece of furniture in that upstairs room. There were a few chairs, but everything else (including kitchen utensils) had to be left on the floor. So far they had three children to look after and, 'God willing', there would certainly be more – rubbish collectors like to have lots of children so that there are more boys to collect the rubbish, and more girls to sort it. Several would die in childhood.

In these circumstances the young man had had little self-respect and had taken to drink and drugs, but now he had met with Christ and felt his love and purifying power. The drink and drugs had gone.

Those things were gone, but what was in their place? My friend pressed him on this point, knowing that while it was not so hard for people to be attracted to Christ, it was much harder for them to stick at the Christian life. For one thing, people don't like rubbish collectors to have any time off, and for another, he couldn't read, so it was hard to feed himself spiritually.

So to answer my friend's question the pig-keeper had to think hard and struggled to find words. He knew he should love his wife, his children, his sister . . .

'And who else?' prodded my friend.

'Everyone?' asked the pig-keeper.

The fact that he even *asked* the question was a sign of the work of the Holy Spirit within him. This area of Cairo had been notorious for fighting, gambling, knifing and shooting incidents. It was not a light thing for someone born and brought up in these circumstances to even consider a different way of life. There were still many barriers and difficulties

to overcome – not the least of which was trying to understand the Christian life when the words of the Arabic Bible
were almost foreign to him.

To try to reinforce the pig-keeper's determination to go
on with Christ, my friend read to him the passage in John
15.1–11 when Jesus talks about the vine and the vinedresser.
But reading anything was for the rubbish collector an alien
activity. My friend found himself in a position rather like
that of a child from school today, trying to explain computer
language to a parent who had never so much as touched a
keyboard. The communication gap was as wide as that.

After every sentence my friend had to ask the pig-keeper
if he understood. If he didn't, he would find another word
and carry on. The aim was that by the end of the conversation the pig-keeper would have a better idea about how
to bear fruit in Christ.

For my lay-worker friend, to have a pig-keeper ask how to
live the Christian life was the greatest miracle that he could
wish for. Knowing the difficulties, knowing the barriers
that had to be overcome – of deprivation, disease, poverty,
ignorance and temptation – this was a far greater miracle
than the more spectacular physical healings and acts of
God that also took place under the rubbish collectors'
mountain. 'Which is easier: to say to the paralytic, "Your
sins are forgiven," or to say, "Get up, take your mat and
walk"?' (Mark 2.9 *NIV*).

In coming to read about the community that lives under
the Muqattam Mountain, you are coming to a mountain of
faith – a place that symbolizes what God can do as he acts
in power to lift up the lowest of the low, to save the weak
to confound the strong.

Cairo landmarks

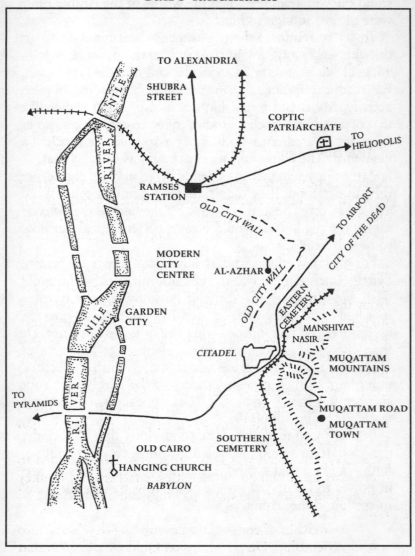

1 WHIRLWIND

The Dustman

A teenage boy with a grimy face stooped under the weight of a tatty wickerwork basket slung over his shoulders. He stopped when he came to a newly occupied flat and hammered on the door. '*Zibaala!*' ('Rubbish!') he called out.

The woman who opened the door caught her breath at the stench of his clothes. Su'aad was a young wife setting up home in Shubra, the district of Cairo that spreads north from the main railway station. It also contains the city's highest concentration of Copts. Su'aad and her husband, Farahat, worked with the Coptic Orthodox Church in their spare time. (To be known as a Copt in modern Egypt is to be identified as a Christian, although it does not necessarily imply any knowledge of Christ or the Christian life.)

Su'aad paid the boy the monthly pittance that he asked for taking their rubbish away. Bit by bit the couple had begun to get to know him as he came to their house almost every day. His name was Qiddees Ageeb. He explained to them how he would go home with his father on a donkey cart and hand over the day's pickings for his mother and sisters to sift.

These snatches of conversation eventually developed into a warm friendship. On one occasion Qiddees asked Farahat

1

what it was like working for a national newspaper, for Farahat was a printer's assistant on *Al-Gumhurriya* (*The Republic*). Although this was a national newspaper, Qiddees had never read it – he was completely illiterate. He then asked Farahat what he did in his spare time.

This opened up the opportunity for Farahat to enthuse about his trips to country villages, for on Sunday mornings he would be up at six to get to services in country churches, after which he and his friends would visit the surrounding neighbourhood. They would then share with the people they met their experience of how Jesus met their needs and transformed their lives.

Qiddees was interested in all this. What could God do in *his* life? Eventually the day came when this teenage boy prayed with Farahat and asked Jesus to change him and turn his life around.

Farahat's Call

After this, whenever Qiddees came to collect the rubbish he used to say to Farahat, 'Come and speak to my people about Christ. The people in our neighbourhood gamble, drink too much, use guns, take drugs – there are so many problems, and there are quarrels and fights every day.'

Initially, Farahat would reply that he was too busy doing outreach work in the villages to visit Qiddees' neighbourhood. This went on for two years, but Qiddees never gave up asking.

One Friday morning in February 1974, Qiddees yet again asked Farahat to go with him to visit the rubbish collectors. This time, though, Farahat heard God's voice clearly saying to him, 'It is I that prepare you, go with him.'

A Modern Jonah

So Farahat told Qiddees that he'd meet him after work that very day, and Qiddees gave him directions to a place called Bab Al-Hadeed, the 'Iron Gate' bus terminus. Farahat now felt in his bones that this really was what God wanted him to do, but his heart was not in it. He was unwilling to change the pattern of service that he was used to, so instead of taking the bus to Bab Al-Hadeed, he decided to get on one going in the opposite direction!

God, though, didn't let him get away with it – any more than he did with Jonah – and Farahat felt God saying to him as he rode on the bus: 'I am the one who is telling you to go. I will be waiting for you at the place Qiddees told you about.'

Farahat felt an inner turmoil, but two stops later made his decision. He got off the bus and caught the next one back to Bab Al-Hadeed. There he found Qiddees waiting for him – completely unaware of Farahat's deliberate detour!

It would be fascinating to know what was going on in Qiddees' mind while he cooled his heels (or rather, in Cairo, '*warmed* his heels'!) waiting for Farahat to turn up. A Western reader will need to view this misdemeanour in an Eastern perspective. Easterners do not see appointments as commitments that must override all other considerations. On the contrary, they can be set aside if something else crops up. A Christian film producer once told me how he'd made an appointment to see another contact in the film industry in Luxor. To reach him he had to drive from Cairo. He got there, but his friend never showed up – and so he drove back to the capital, a round trip of 500 miles. When they next met up, neither of them made any reference whatsoever to the missed appointment!

So whatever Qiddees' feelings were about Farahat's late arrival, he quickly got on with the job of guiding him to his destination. He took Farahat into the middle of the vast cemetery on the eastern edge of Cairo. In this part of the world, families who own tombs build them like houses and bury their dead in vaults under the floor. Foreigners call the cemetery 'The City of the Dead', yet homeless people and refugees live in the tombs, renting the upper storeys. So Farahat and Qiddees' evening walk, eerie as it might have been among the shadows, was not a lonely one.

When they finally reached the other side, Farahat felt as if he'd entered a living hell. He could hardly believe his senses. It wasn't just the stench. To some extent, Qiddees had prepared him for the tin shacks, the filthy animals and the heaps of rubbish, but he'd never imagined that such a 'God-forsaken' place could be thronging with such a seething mass of humanity. In the first street they came to, hundreds of children were milling around with men and women of all ages. Farahat had never met more than seventy-five Copts in any town he had served in, and in some villages there were only four or five. But here in one street there were hundreds.

Farahat felt his heart pounding. He hardly knew where to begin. 'Where do you worship?' he asked one man.

'We don't worship.'

'Do you know about Christ?'

'No.'

'All right,' said Farahat, 'but first we need a place to worship in.'

The man said, 'There is one place you could use – it's really a grotto.'

So Farahat promised him, 'I will come to you on Sunday very early, and you can take me to this grotto.'

4

This time, Farahat was as good as his word, and at six o'clock the following Sunday morning he went up the mountainside and the people led him into the 'grotto'. This turned out to be a gap beneath a massive rock that must have weighed several thousand tons. There Farahat held services on the next three Sundays.

The Whirlwind's Manifesto

On the third Sunday, another lay-worker called Fayid joined Farahat. There were some 14,000 Copts living in an area of around 4 square kilometres – so Farahat was more than grateful for some help in visiting them. Farahat and Fayid went up to the grotto and prayed together. Farahat prayed aloud, 'Lord, I'm just a drop in the ocean. There are very many people here and they are very hard, wild people. What do you want from me? Do you want me to start a school, a Sunday school, a society, or a church? I don't know – tell me!'

Hardly were the words out of his mouth, when a sand-storm blew up. Violent gusts of wind came howling up the mountain. Farahat and Fayid were about halfway up on a narrow plateau. There were people below them and cliffs above them. The wind whipped up all the papers in the rubbish below them and flung them high into the sky. In a few seconds, blizzards of paper soared towards the highest of the mountain peaks.

In the resulting chaos one piece of paper fluttered down in front of Farahat. Fayid bent down and picked it up. 'Look at this,' he said. 'What's this piece of paper?' Farahat took it and, to his surprise, found it was a page from the Bible. His eye immediately fell on the verse that says, 'One night, Paul had a vision, and in it the Lord said, "Don't be afraid to keep on preaching. Don't stop! I am with you, and you won't be harmed. Many people in this city belong to me"' (Acts 18.9–10). To this day, Farahat has kept this piece of paper with him.

At this point Farahat really began to sense that God wanted to do something, but he still didn't know exactly what. In the Coptic Church it is common to go to an older priest, or 'father confessor', for spiritual guidance. Farahat had just such a longstanding relationship with Father Zakariya Butros (or Zechariah Peter), so he went and told this priest what he and Fayid faced in this new area of ministry. But it wasn't the actual advice he gave that made its mark on Farahat. What impressed him most was the inspiration Father Zakariya derived from God's promise to Joshua – a subject that he often preached about.

This promise had come to Farahat when he stood with Fayid on the edge of the district: 'Every place that the sole of your foot will tread upon I have given to you' (Joshua 1.3 *RSV*). As Fayid walked around looking for a suitable site for ministry, Farahat in simple faith set the sole of his foot on the spot where he was standing.

Fayid did not know what was going on in Farahat's mind. The pair met again as they completed their circuits. Finding Farahat standing facing the opposite way, Fayid asked him what he was doing. Farahat's reply took him by surprise.

'Didn't God say to Joshua, "I will give you every place where you set your foot?"'

Farahat felt sure this was where God wanted a church. So after marking out the site, they soon embarked on the building of a corrugated iron hut. They roofed it in reeds, in the local style. That first meeting-place reminded them of the stable in Bethlehem, but to the rubbish collectors it was a tin home just like theirs. It was only 170 square metres in area.

Eleven children came to the first Sunday school and nine adults to the first open meeting, held on 13 April 1974. But slowly the numbers began to grow until there was no room for all the children who came to worship.

Believing in the importance of providing the children with an education as well as pastoral care, Farahat's wife Su'aad opened two kindergarten classes in 1975. It was a simple beginning, but held the promise of expansion in the future. The adult meetings grew to the point where the iron hut was filled to overflowing. So they decided to do away with the tin sheets and instead build a small church of brick. But before starting to build the second church, they took a good look at the first to see how they could improve on it. They employed plasterers and fitted red stained glass to create a pleasant decor that would encourage more people to come. But they made the roof from canvas, which gave the feeling of being inside the Tabernacle or Tent of Meeting.

Farahat's spiritual guide, Father Zakariya, took him to see the Coptic Patriarch, Pope Shenouda, who encouraged them a great deal with many Bible verses. They explained to the Patriarch that they wanted to build a more substantial roof for the church. (In Egypt, the Patriarch is a political figure as well as a religious one – his influence is vital in getting permission to build or extend a church.) The Patriarch agreed to start up a fund for a concrete roof. Yet the rate at which the attendance at the church shot up amazed them – even the new place was now too small.

By the time Father Zakariya had raised the money for the second roof it was already time to be thinking about a *third* building. So Farahat prayed, 'Lord, we need another roof and the first cost 90 pounds, and the second was 96 pounds. To do the roof for the third place in concrete will cost *1,000* pounds. This, Lord, is a very large sum of money.'

Yet Farahat felt God was saying to him, 'I told you I have many people in this town, so the place must be very spacious to take in the new people.' So they went ahead with the plans for the next church.

Father Zakariya found a really good architect and they marked out a site of 1,000 square metres. Each day, Farahat used to come straight from his job at the newspaper and join the labourers in shifting piles of rubbish to widen the space for the church. Local people looking on could see that everyone involved in the project was pulling together.

While they worked on this latest church there was still plenty of visiting and follow-up to do. Farahat was puzzled, though, to meet people in the street, who suddenly looked shocked and ran home – he just couldn't fathom the reason. In fact, his mere presence was spiritually challenging to the people, disturbing their sinful lifestyle. All Farahat knew was that God had said to him, 'I have people in this town.' So Farahat felt God would bring in the people. But he couldn't deny that the vision was there, and the promise, 'Don't be afraid . . . I am with you, and you won't be harmed' (Acts 18.9–10).

Evangelistic Athletics

In this same year, 1974, one of the believers had a vision. He saw a desk, and in front of that desk all the people of Egypt. It was easy enough for Farahat to interpret this as a vision of evangelism, but when he actually set about evangelizing he found the Holy Spirit leading him to do things that he had no experience of at all.

Many of the Copts had never heard of Christ and didn't want to listen to what Farahat had to say. Often he knocked at doors, only to find that no one would answer them.

'OK, so what's the matter? Why is everyone hiding?' he would shout out. If he did get into a house, he often found people sitting around drinking. They would then take one look at him and run away. Yet Farahat felt the Holy Spirit was saying, 'Run after them!'

'Is *this* what evangelism is?' he asked himself, as he hared after them, gasping for breath to keep up. In the end, Farahat decided persistence was the answer, so he kept up the chase until he actually caught one of the fugitives! On one occasion he caught up with someone carrying a big carafe of spirits, so he grabbed hold of him and brought him that same day to a church meeting. The man then began a new life in Christ and the carafe went into a special museum the church keeps of things given up by people who have repented!

Once when Farahat was out visiting with Samir, another volunteer, they went into a house to invite people to a meeting. They were sitting down eating in the dark. One of them said, 'My name is Ali, and as I'm a Muslim, I won't be going. These others are Christians – take them along.'

The religious scruples of the man who called himself Ali may have prevented him from attending a Christian meeting, but his scruples were certainly not of the stringent kind. To most Muslims, drinking any alcohol is a sin that could send you to the 'fires of hell' – yet unseen by his visitors, Ali was all the time quietly sipping from a carafe of strong spirits.

In the darkness Farahat and Samir couldn't make out the people very well. So they stood up to go, but someone said,

'You wanted to meet together, so stay and eat with us.'

'All right,' they replied, 'but we like to pray before we eat.'

They stood up to pray, and during the prayer there came a shriek – and a sound that struck like a bombshell. Someone had grabbed a big bottle of alcohol and smashed it. It was the man who had called himself Ali Muslim, who had a huge moustache and only one eye. Suddenly he cried out, 'God forgive me, I have denied you. I am a criminal and a killer – and I am now coming back to you.' It turned out that his real name was Shawqy Zaki. He came to the meeting and made a commitment to the Lord that very night.

The more that Farahat learned about Shawqy, the more he saw that he was a remarkable example of God's grace. In his past life he couldn't bear to pass a day without a quarrel or fight. And if no quarrel came up in the ordinary course of events, he would go out and start one. Once he went out and hailed a taxi. He then embarked on a grand tour of Cairo, keeping the driver going well into the night. At last they came back to their starting point and the driver asked for his fare. To his horror, he found himself looking at the blade of Shawqy's knife and ran away. This was in fact one of the *mildest* of Shawqy's excesses, in a life in which violence predominated.

One day, driven to distraction by his failure to find someone to fight with, Shawqy decided to turn his anger inwards and stabbed himself in the stomach with a sharp knife. Bleeding heavily, he was rushed to hospital and survived. What was even worse was the effect that these outbursts of violence had on his family. The worst example of this was when he deliberately set fire to his house. Inside were his wife and nine children. They survived, but in his crazy career of theft and violence Shawqy had twice killed people. This was the kind of man whose life Christ turned around that night through Farahat's courageous outreach.

Early in Farahat's ministry to the rubbish collectors he felt the Spirit was giving him some practical advice: 'Don't just wade into all that mud, paper and waste. Get some boots and tuck your trousers into them.' Farahat was sure this was clear guidance from God, so he got the boots immediately. Since the people he was trying to reach kept running away from him, he had to learn to tuck his trousers in and run after them. More and more, Farahat was realizing that successful evangelism in this area involved going in for sport: to reach people, Farahat had to become an athlete!

One night someone Farahat wanted to invite to a service hid himself in the middle of a pig-pen! How on earth was he going to reach the man among the pigs, the offal and other horrors? The answer, Farahat realized, was to add a torch to the boots that were already part of his essential outreach kit. So at the next opportunity Farahat found his way into the pig-pen and shone the torch on his quarry! The man was frightened by the light and was cowering in a box. So Farahat went in and persuaded him to come out.

However, Farahat was not always so relentless, like some hunter with his prey. If someone refused an invitation to a meeting, Farahat might simply reply, 'Never mind, I'm sorry if I disturbed you.'

There were also gentler forms of persuasion. In Egypt close friends of the same sex may greet each other by kissing on both cheeks. At an Egyptian wedding a male guest will never kiss the bride, but if he is a friend of the bridegroom they may kiss on both cheeks and embrace for some time. So to kiss someone you have just been arguing with is a radical thing to do. It is not just a gambit to patch up a quarrel: it means that you are claiming his friendship. But if the professional from the church does the kissing, this is completely back to front. It is always the ordinary rank-and-file Coptic lay people who kiss the hand of the priest, never the other way round. Again Farahat found the Holy Spirit leading him down a different path to custom and tradition.

Confronted with a man who refused to come to a meeting, he found God saying to him, 'Kiss his hand, kiss his hand!' He did, and the man got up to go with him. Another man wouldn't budge. God seemed to be saying to Farahat, 'Kiss his head!' By this time, Farahat was thinking 'Whatever next!' However, he did it anyway, and the second man struggled to his feet. A third man was still obstinate, but the Spirit prompted Farahat, 'Pick up his shoe and put it on for him.' Farahat bent down and looked around for the shoe, found it, and put it on the man. The man gave a jolt, then jumped up and followed Farahat to the meeting.

Such was the variety of evangelistic methods prompted by the Holy Spirit in Farahat's ministry – one minute haring after someone, the next being urged to grovel!

Healing the Healer

So Farahat slowly discovered that there is a kind of evangelism that does not depend on human methods or on following the customs that have been handed down to us. It is an evangelism led by the Holy Spirit. Once, he was called in to pray for someone. There was no electricity in the area at that time, and Farahat couldn't see the person very well. He didn't know what was wrong with him, but when Farahat had prayed, the man shouted out, 'My eyes are opened. I was blind and now I can see!'

Farahat had no idea that the man was blind. He asked him to point to things in the room:

'What's this?'

'A towel.'

'What's this?'

'A lady', and so on.

It was very clear the man had been healed.

For such a dynamic ministry Farahat needed to be fit. Yet the smells and the smoke from one visit could make him ill for a week. Millions of scraps of rubbish attracted millions of scavenging insects. One family invited Farahat to share a meal with them, oblivious to the flies massing on the table. Yet to refuse to eat with them would have been unthinkable.

Although the people were poor and their lives surrounded by rubbish and dirt, they couldn't wash their faces more than once a week. There was barely enough water to drink, and there were no amenities of any kind. Tap water and electricity were undreamt-of luxuries.

After a while, Farahat found that when he slept he started to ooze blood. Every time he shifted position in his sleep blood would seep out of him. The doctor told him to stay in his bed in Shubra and not to return to the rubbish collectors in Manshiyat Nasir and the many infections that were there. He followed this advice for a while and the blood flow stopped, but he didn't have peace about this decision. There was a restlessness inside him, which made him realize that he couldn't be happy if he abandoned the rubbish collectors.

So although he was still ill Farahat went back to them. He was still so weak that someone had to carry him on his shoulder and lay him down inside the meeting house. He slept, but he couldn't move. So he said to God, 'Lord, today you've got to give me a boost. How can I lie here when souls are dying out there?'

While he was still sleeping, a power seized hold of him. The sensation startled him into wakefulness. Gingerly, he began to move again – and found he could get up. He immediately ran outside and started visiting the people again and bringing them to the meetings.

The illness never returned.

2 A MOUNTAIN TO MOVE

Move! Move!

Farahat realized that he needed to know more about the people of the mountain – how they had come to be there, etc. – so he could learn to serve them better. Very little of their history was known in the outside world.

The presidency of Gemal Abdul Nasir (1956–1970) was well known for social upheavals and movements of population. The most famous was his decision to move the Nubian people off their land. This was to make way for the Aswan High Dam that was to provide electricity from the south of Egypt.

The Nubians had struggled for centuries to defend their language, their customs and culture from outside pressures. Unlike the Copts, they succeeded in keeping their language alive to this day. Their customs include giving their children 'the baptism of John'. But with no Church of their own, Christianity never took deep root among them. The Arabs cut them off from the Coptic Church and their faith faded away.

Nasir moved them off their homelands to make way for the dam lake, Lake Nasir. He put many of them in a complex of villages near Aswan called Medinat Nasir, or 'Nasir City'. But while all this was going on, the world's media missed another movement of population around the same time – the decision to move thousands of low-income Copts to Manshiyat Nasir, or 'Nasir Suburb'.[1] This was a barren site on the lower slopes of the Muqattam Mountain.

The *Zeballeen* Story

During the centuries of Islamic rule that led up to the modern period, Egyptians who did not convert to Islam had to pay for the privilege of remaining Copts. Those who could afford to do so were probably wealthy, but it was not until 1855 that this special *gezyah* tax was lifted. By then, with the constant burden of extra taxation, many Copts had become very poor. As a result, some became *zeballeen* – slum dwellers who carted away the rubbish of the various towns that came to comprise Cairo.

The people we now know as *zeballeen* can be divided into two separate social groups. Those who were first on the scene came about a hundred years ago from the oases of Egypt. They collected household waste and sold what they could to be used as fuel for heating public baths or for cooking beans in oil. In the end, they became middlemen who sold on these recycled products.

This change of status happened as the second social group appeared on the scene. Landless peasants, mostly from Christian families, migrated to Cairo from the south. They took over the job of collecting household waste, under the supervision of the people from the oases who were there first. Their Muslim supervisors were forbidden by Islamic law to touch pork or come into contact with pigs, but as Christians the newcomers were free to do this. Therefore they could supplement their income by keeping pigs that were fed on the food scraps.

There are seven *zeballeen* districts around Greater Cairo. The largest of these is Manshiyat Nasir, which was created in 1969 when the Governor of Cairo had thousands of rubbish collectors moved to the east of the city on to the lower slopes of the Muqattam Mountain. These low-income Copts had been moved on at least once before, but in Manshiyat Nasir (New Nasir Suburb) there were no buildings at all and no services. The newcomers did not even have time to plan or prepare the area. They had to get to work immediately on bringing in the rubbish, so any attempts they made to build for themselves were very haphazard. When they did find the time, they turned their hands to levelling the ground and building tin shacks on it, with pig-pens attached to them.

Some 7,000 rubbish collectors get up at the crack of dawn every morning at Manshiyat Nasir. They go to blocks of flats, hotels and other parts of Cairo and collect over 2,000 tons of rubbish. They take this home, emptying their carts in the backyard or in front of their shacks. The women and older girls sort the rubbish into organic and inorganic refuse, and the edible leftovers go to their pigs and cattle. They then sort the durable waste materials according to type and colour.

The rubbish collectors gather the secondary materials such as glass, paper, plastic, tin, rags and bones into big bundles in front of their dwellings. They then sell them to the middlemen from the oases, who come with their vehicles to collect them. In turn, the middlemen sell them to factories for recycling.

Any waste that couldn't be reused, such as the refuse from the animal enclosures, they used to leave on the paths. Eventually it would be burnt or sent to the incinerator or the rubbish tip in the lower part of the area. Understandably, the living conditions were deplorable, and there was a very real danger of fire breaking out as a result of spontaneous combustion from materials reacting together in the remaining refuse. When such explosions did occur, they put both the environment and people's health at risk, as did the pall of thick black smoke that settled over a large part of the area.

It was into this scene of poverty and spiritual deprivation that God had called the young man Farahat Ibrahim.

Manager of *Al-Kiraza* Press

By this time, Farahat was facing a very difficult time at work; and as he could find no way to cope with the problems he faced, in 1976 he went to the Patriarch, Pope Shenouda, for advice. Seeing that Farahat was unsettled in his job at the newspaper, Pope Shenouda saw a golden opportunity to turn his talents to good use for the Church. 'Don't put up with it!' he declared. 'Stay with me.'[2]

So it was that Farahat found himself called to leave his job with *The Republic* newspaper and instead serve under the Patriarch's direct supervision. Pope Shenouda appointed him manager of the *Al-Kiraza* or 'Proclamation' Press. Among the tasks of this press was to print regularly *Al-Kiraza*, the official magazine of the Orthodox Church. Working directly under the Patriarch's supervision was to Farahat a tremendous privilege, and one that gave him great insight into a life lived in full-time commitment to ministry. Sometimes he would see Pope Shenouda staying up into the small hours of the morning to meet some deadline or other. This encouraged Farahat to emulate such commitment to Christian service – rather than finding any excuse not to!

Beauty for Ashes

The most momentous event of 1976 in Manshiyat Nasir was the fire that swept through the entire district. Yet the wholesale destruction it caused paved the way for a process of transformation. The residents gradually began to use local stone for building, instead of the scrap tin and corrugated iron sheets. They stuck to the original plan of their homes – one big room for living and working in, and an enclosure for animals attached to it. A corrugated iron fence separated the pig-pens from the household. An office for environmental change also emerged, which worked with engineering consultants to plan and name the streets of the district. The result was the first meaningful map of the area, and it gave the residents the beginnings of a sense of security. With the rebuilding of their dwellings, they filed claims for ownership of the land with the local government.

At the same time as the residents were rebuilding their homes, so the time seemed ripe to build a permanent church in this residential area below the mountain.

Farahat had wanted to be a minister in many places, including Sudan, yet he was very certain that God was calling him to be a minister in one specific church. The Muqattam church was being built from scratch. One day when Farahat was sitting with a friend, a man came up to them and announced to Farahat: 'I tell you that you will be the priest of this church and you will be the one to give it the name of Simaan.'

This man was uneducated, knowing neither how to read nor to write, yet he knew when God was speaking to him. Once in a Bible meeting, he knew the Lord was clearly speaking to him about his addiction to smoking.

Immediately the man promised to repent and threw away all the tobacco he had in his pocket. But when he got home he found his niece waiting for him. She held out her hand to him, clutching something in it. 'Look what I've found, Uncle,' she said, expecting him to be very pleased with her. 'It's your tobacco – I found it in the church!'

Although this humble prophet had informed Farahat that he would be the priest of the church, such an idea was still far from his thoughts. Farahat didn't have the qualifications that the job demanded and being a *khaadim* (lay-worker) seemed more than enough to be getting on with. But God seemed to have other plans and gave him a vision. Farahat saw himself entering a vast church that was to be built in Muqattam. In front of him he saw a tall rock blocking his path, but God flattened the rock and Farahat kept going and entered the huge church. Farahat felt this vision was a clear sign that it was God's plan that he would be there in the future. Yet he didn't breathe a word of this to anyone. God seemed to be giving Farahat a firm assurance that he wanted to use him – but Farahat felt equally strongly that he didn't deserve it.

Meanwhile, on the morning of 18 June 1976, the Patriarch paid a surprise visit to the area.[3] He was thrilled with the progress on the church building. He also climbed up to the cavern on the mountainside. There wasn't time for him to get right up to the top of the mountain, yet he could see its potential as a centre for worship, and as he went up he chanted Psalm 24: 'Who may ascend the hill of the LORD? Who may stand in his holy place? He who has clean hands and a pure heart, who does not lift up his soul to an idol or swear by what is false. He will receive blessing from the LORD and vindication from God his Saviour' (24.3–6).

To Farahat, this was a fulfilment of the word that he had received from Joshua 1.3, 'I will give you every place where you set your foot.' He felt very blessed and encouraged by the visit, which the Patriarch made with Farahat's own spiritual counsellor, Father Zakariya Butros.

Soon after, Farahat went to see Father Zakariya, and as they were talking the older man mentioned that he was going to call the new church 'the Church of the Virgin'. But Farahat felt strongly that God was saying to him, 'Call it St Simaan Al-Khiraaz ['St Simaan the Tanner'], for it was because of him that this mountain moved. The mountain belongs to the church of St Simaan Al-Khiraaz and the miracle took place through him.' So Farahat explained to Zakariya Butros that he felt God had spoken to him, and the two men agreed that the church should be called the 'Church of Simaan Al-Khiraaz'.

The First Caliph

Farahat later discovered that Simaan the Tanner had lived 1,000 years ago in the period when for the first time the ruler of Egypt claimed to be the 'caliph' or leader of all the Muslims.

This ruler invaded Egypt from the west at a time when the country was weakened by natural disasters. As the country has very little rain, the farmers depended on the annual flooding of the Nile to grow their crops. The flood fell short three years in a row. The devastating famine that followed led to the spread of epidemics, and whole dioceses just 'faded out of existence'.[4] Altogether 'more than half a million people' died.[5]

In the chaos, rebellion broke out in a city called Tanis, on the north-eastern edge of the Nile delta. The rebels plundered Christian dwellings and forced women and girls away from their homes. This went on until the children of a Copt called Qashlan managed to contact the new government and get them to put a stop to the insurrections.[6]

The Copts now found themselves free to work in a whole range of crafts and professions. These included carpentry, furniture-making, metalwork and shipbuilding. They even held services 'on the decks of their boats and at the ports officially',[7] because the shipyard workers and the craftsmen – and even the sailors – were Copts.

This was the beginning of the Fatimid rule in Egypt. The Fatimids were the first Muslim rulers of Egypt to claim the title of Caliph, or God's regent on earth. The first Caliph was Al-Mui'z Li Din Illah (the name means Upholder of the Religion of God). He had two passions: one was religious debate, and the other was his project to build himself a new capital called Al-Qahirah (the Victorious) or – in English – Cairo.

We now use the term 'Old Cairo' to describe some built-up areas that already existed before the Caliph began his new city. Old Cairo covers parts of the capitals of the Muslim rulers that came before him. It also includes the even older town of Babylon. This had sprung up around a Roman fortress. Suspended over the two bastions of the Roman Gate is '*Al-Kenissa Al-Mu' allaqah*' or 'The Hanging Church'. It is so old that some of its beams date back to before Christ. Many churches in the area testify that Jesus lived there as a boy after his flight from Herod (Matthew 2.13–14, 19). Others, such as the Church of St Barbara, commemorate Christians martyred under the Romans.

The Caliph Al-Mui'z founded his new city of Cairo in the year 969. Its centre was to cover more or less the same district until the middle of the nineteenth century. At its heart lay the Al-Azhar mosque, originally built for the teaching of Islam in its Isma'ili form. Close to it was the shrine of Husayn, son of the fourth Caliph, 'Ali, and his wife Fatima, the Prophet's daughter.

The Fatimids claimed to be descended from both Fatima and 'Ali. Being of the Isma'ili sect, their teaching was in some ways like the Shi'is of modern Iran. They believed that God sends leaders for every period in history, and since God is guiding these rulers they cannot make mistakes. The Fatimids claimed not only to be the caliphs (political leaders) of the Muslim community, but also the *imams* (religious leaders). But the first Caliph did not claim full divine authority. Indeed, he was more tolerant than many of his contemporaries. He encouraged Muslim, Christian and Jewish teachers to debate controversial issues in his presence, on the condition that they did this without anger or contention.[8]

The Debate

Yet not all those around the Caliph were of the same spirit. In his retinue was an ambitious man called Ibn Killis, who had been a vizier (government minister) under the previous regime. When the Fatimids came, he had changed sides, and helped to contribute to the downfall of his previous masters. He had also converted to Islam to boost his chances of getting back his post as a government minister. Ibn Killis had a rival for this job whom he feared would be preferred to him. This was Ibn Mina, who everyone called 'the Fortunate One'.

Ibn Mina was a Christian who was not willing to convert to Islam for the sake of obtaining high office. So Ibn Killis decided to exploit this point by challenging the

Christians to a debate. He appointed a Jew named Moses to debate for him against the then Coptic Patriarch, Abraam. Abraam appointed a learned bishop called Anba Sawirus to take up the challenge. In the debate, Sawirus stung Moses by quoting against him his own prophet.

'It is Isaiah . . . who said about you, "The ox knows his master, the donkey his owner's manger, but Israel does not know, my people do not understand"' (Isaiah 1.3 *NIV*). When the Caliph heard confirmation from Moses' own lips that these really were the words of his prophet, he laughed aloud. Moses and his sponsor, Ibn Killis, were furious at being made to look foolish in front of their ruler. They considered how to take their revenge.

After some thought, they found a verse in the Gospel of Matthew that they could use as a weapon (17.20).

The Ultimatum

Ibn Killis and Moses went to the Caliph. They declared, 'We have found it written in the book of the Christians that whosoever has faith as small as a mustard seed can move a mountain. So it is our right to demand that they prove their religion right by this means. If they cannot, they should be punished for the invalidity of their religion.'

Mulling it over, the Caliph decided that here was a golden opportunity to improve the prospects for his new capital. If the Christians really could move mountains, then let them do so and clear a space for the expansion of his new city! And if they could not, then that would provide proof that their religion was wrong and should be abolished.

Therefore the Caliph sent for Patriarch Abraam and presented him with the following ultimatum for all Christians. They must fulfil the gospel teaching by moving the eastern part of the Muqattam Mountain. If they failed, they would have to choose one of three penalties: first, they could convert to Islam on the basis that Christianity was invalid; second, they could leave Egypt and emigrate to another country; or third, the whole Coptic community would be put to the sword.

3 EARTHQUAKE

The Patriarch's Reply

This challenge came like a bolt from the blue, ten years into a reign that had become one of relative peace and security for the Copts. The Patriarch was stunned into silence, and prayed that God would give him the wisdom to know how to reply. After sending up this 'arrow prayer', he then asked for, and was granted, three days' grace before giving his answer. He immediately called on all Christians in Egypt to fast for three days from dawn till sunset and to pray fervently for the Church's deliverance from this ordeal.

The Patriarch then went to the Hanging Church in Babylon (still to be found in what is now called 'Old Cairo') and summoned there all the bishops, archdeacons and monks in the vicinity. He told them, 'We must fast and pray for three days, so that the Lord may show mercy upon us in his grace, and provide us a way of deliverance.'

So fasting and vigils began in earnest throughout Egypt, and all the Copts who heard the call prayed for deliverance from the ordeal ahead. At dawn on the third day, when the Patriarch was due to give his answer to the Caliph, he had a dream. According to Coptic tradition, the Virgin Mary appeared to him in it and said, 'What is the matter with you?'

The Patriarch answered, 'You know what it is, lady of the heavenly and earthly beings.'

In reply, she said, 'Fear not, faithful shepherd . . . for your tears which you have shed in this church, and the fasts and prayers which you and your people have offered up shall not be forgotten. Now, get out through the iron gate that leads to the market-place and, when you are on your way out, you will find a one-eyed man in front of you carrying a water skin. Take hold of him; for he is the man by whom the miracle will take place.'

Simaan the Tanner

As soon as the Patriarch awoke, he went out through the iron gate and found the man spoken of in the dream. He took him inside, closing the gate behind them. Then he told him everything that had happened, the Caliph's ultimatum, and the dream that had revealed by whom the miracle would take place.

The stranger looked puzzled, then replied, 'Forgive me, my father, for I am but a sinful man.'

But the Patriarch persisted and insisted that this was a heavenly command. On hearing this, the man submitted. The Patriarch asked him his name. He answered:

'My name is Simaan the Tanner. I work in tanning animal skins. But I wake up early every day to fill a skin with water to give to those who can't fetch it for themselves because of old age or illness.

'When I have done this, I return my water skin to the house and go to my work at the tannery where I work till evening. And at sunset I go out with the others and eat just enough to keep myself alive. Then I turn to prayer . . .'

Simaan insisted that while he was still alive the Patriarch

should not tell anyone who he was, or anything about his role in the ordeal to come.

Suddenly it seemed as if Simaan knew what God was asking of him. He said, 'My honourable father, go up the mountain and take along with you the religious leaders, the deacons, and the archdeacons. Make them carry on high the Bibles, the crosses, and the long candles, these being lit, and the censers full of incense.

'And ask the king and his retinue to go up with you. You must stand on one side of the mountain, while they stand on the side opposite you. As for me, I will stand among the people, so no one will recognize me.

'Then, after administering the holy sacraments, raise up your voice with all of the people, repeating, '*Kyrie Eleison*' ('Lord, have mercy') 400 times.

'Then, after that, keep silent for some moments, and worship, you and the priests, before the Most High. Repeat this three times, and every time you stand up after worshipping, draw the sign of the cross over the mountain, and you shall see the glory of God.'

Power Encounter

The Patriarch prayed a prayer of thanksgiving to God, who had allowed the trial to come, but was providing a way out.[1] He then told the Caliph that he was ready to carry out his request by the grace of God.

The Caliph rode out with several important men of his retinue, and all his soldiers. He met the Patriarch, along with many bishops, priests, deacons, archdeacons and laity. Among the laity, of course, was Simaan the Tanner. The two parties took up their positions on the mountain facing each other.

The Patriarch and the bishops lifted up the sacraments

and administered them. The people then repeated the *Kyrie Eleison* prayer 400 times: 100 towards the east, then the west, the north and the south. After this, they remained silent, placing themselves at God's mercy.

The people then began to worship. While the Patriarch drew the sign of the cross, they bowed down to the ground and then arose again. And as they did this, a great earthquake convulsed the mountain. Each time the people bowed down, the mountain was thrust down, and each time they stood up, the mountain was raised up so that the rays of the sun could be seen shining through underneath it.

This happened three times, the mountain crashing down and rising up as the people prostrated themselves and stood up again. The Caliph was overcome with awe and fear, as were all his followers. He cried out at the top of his voice, 'God is great; may his name be blessed!' and he begged the Patriarch to stop what he was doing, for fear his city would be completely destroyed.

When calm finally descended on the scene, the Caliph confessed to the Patriarch, 'You have proved that your faith is a true one.'

And so it was that the mountain, the surface of which was originally level and connected, became divided into three parts leaving space between them. The Arabic dictionaries say that the word *muqattam* means 'cut up'. The Caliph had the space to enlarge his new capital, but the miracle had profoundly affected him.

First, he asked the Patriarch privately what he could do for him. The Patriarch answered wisely, 'The only thing I ask is that the Lord may lengthen your span of life, and give you victory over your enemies.'

But the Caliph insisted on granting a favour, so the Patriarch said, 'All right, since you press me, I would dearly love permission to be granted for the church of Saint Markorios Abu Seifeyn to be rebuilt, for it has been torn down and what was left used as a storehouse for sugar-cane. Also, I would like the walls of the Hanging Church to be restored, for they are now cracked.'

The Caliph immediately drew up a decree authorizing the repairs and even offered to pay for them out of the State treasury. Yet the Patriarch politely refused the money, saying that God would provide. And indeed this was the beginning of a new age of church building and renewal throughout Egypt.

This was all done with the active support of the Caliph. When his decree authorizing the repairs was issued, mobs gathered outside the church of Abu Seifeyn, which was in Babylon, Old Cairo. 'Abu Seifeyn' literally means 'father of two swords' and is a name given to Saint Markorios, to whom the church was dedicated. Markorios came to know Christ while serving as a soldier in the Roman army. According to Coptic tradition, God appeared to him in a vision and encouraged him. In addition to the sword he carried as a soldier, God gave him a divine sword to wield for him. Markorios was eventually martyred in God's cause.

The mob was in no mood, however, to see a Christian martyr honoured, and were determined to stop the rebuilding. But in the event, they found 'God's sword' wielded against them. When the news of the mob reached the Caliph, he was furious, and rode his horse into Babylon at the head of his army. There he ordered the builders to work in his presence, and under his own supervision. The mob was dumbfounded by this demonstration of the Caliph's determination.

Indeed it was whispered in some quarters that the Caliph had become a Christian. According to Coptic records, he was indeed secretly baptized in the great baptistry for adult immersion which is still to be seen at the church of Abu Seifeyn. Soon afterwards, though, he handed over power to his son and disappeared.

Again, according to Coptic sources, no official announcement of his death was made until at least six months after the event. The circumstances that surround it are shrouded in mystery.

Adham's Head

Clearly it was part of God's design to use the name of St Simaan as a source of inspiration for the present-day ministry in Muqattam. It seemed only right, therefore, to expect God to work just as powerfully for his glory as he had done in answer to the prayers of Simaan the Tanner in the tenth century.

One very wonderful thing happened even in the building of the church itself. They could get cement and sand and metal, but there was no water available. In fact, there was not a single source of water in the whole area. People would buy water from below the mountain, but it took half a day to fetch it.

A month later all the materials were ready and waiting – except for the water. One day after worship, Farahat went out on the Muqattam road and found a tractor pulling a water tanker near the roads up to Muqattam. Farahat was sure that God was saying to him, 'Go in here and he will give you water for the church.'

So he went up to the tractor driver and said, 'Can you help us? We're building a church and we need water.'

'Go and see Abd Al-Kareem, the engineer,' said the tractor driver. 'He's in charge.'

Kareem? This name surprised Farahat. In the form it was given, it was a non-Christian name, but Copts also used it to mean 'generous'. Perhaps it was auspicious after all. Farahat felt that God was insisting, so he entered the hut and greeted the engineer. 'Good evening,' the man responded. But Farahat simply blurted out, 'We're building a church and we need water.'

'*Min ayneya!*' Kareem responded. Literally this means, 'from my two eyes', and in practice is a promise that the service requested will be granted. 'Our premises are up in Muqattam and this is the address,' he said to Farahat. 'Build a cistern to take water and we will send you the tractor with the water-tanker.'

Farahat could hardly believe that the problem was finally being solved. So he went and found a type of chamber in the hill and sealed it up. It had the capacity for 70 cubic metres of water. Next he contacted the organization and immediately they sent three tractors with water-tankers to fill the cistern.

By the beginning of 1977 they had reached the stage of constructing the second storey of the church building, and on 19 January Farahat was due to preach at an evening service. After finishing work that day, he went to the church and asked how the work was getting on. The reply shocked him.

'Adham is dying in the Al-Azhar hospital.'

'Who is Adham?' he asked. (Adham means Adam.)

It turned out that Adham was one of the builders and had met with a tragic accident on the site. They explained what had happened: 'A tractor was backing up and he was sitting between the tractor and the tanker. He fell off and the wheel crushed his head.'

This news shocked Farahat deeply. Why should someone

be killed for building a church? It didn't seem possible. He then said, 'Today we will neither preach nor sing. We will do only one thing – pray. What is that chair made from?'

'Wood,' one worshipper responded, looking puzzled.

'If it broke, what would we do about it?'

'We would mend it with wood.'

'Who would mend it?' he asked.

'The carpenter.'

Farahat said, 'Adham was made from dust. So who made him?'

'Our Lord.'

Farahat summed up. 'That's all there is to it, then. We need to say to our Lord, "Please mend his head – or make him a new one!"'

The people of Muqattam were very confused as to how this could happen, but when it came to the word of the Lord, they believed it.

So Farahat sent for a doctor to visit Adham in the hospital. But when the doctor saw Adham, he pronounced: 'There's no chance of him recovering. Nothing short of a miracle could save him now.'

Yet the doctor himself was to be greatly helped in his spiritual life by what followed. Three days later Farahat went to the hospital with some companions and found Adham still in a coma. In fact, he looked like a corpse. The tractor wheel had squashed his head just about flat, so it looked like the local bread – more in the shape of pitta bread than a farmhouse loaf! Blood was trickling out of his nostrils, mouth and ears. His eyes had almost disappeared into his head. Farahat was horrified by the severity of Adham's injuries.

With tears pouring down their faces, they prayed there and then in the heart of the hospital. 'Lord, you are the one who made Adham's head and you can create a new head. You are the God of miracles and wonders.'

At that moment, there was a very slight stirring; it was just enough to show that life was still present. Then they left.

Precisely nine days after the accident, the church workers asked Adham's friends how he was getting on. 'He's at home,' they replied.

'At *home*?' they questioned incredulously.

'Yes.'

So they went to his house, and found Adham asleep on a mat. He had recovered sufficiently to be playing with his children. Yet his new head was noticeably larger than the old one. God really had worked a miracle.

This particular miracle gave a big boost to God's work in building the church. It enabled Farahat and his team to finish the second storey of the church, spurred on by enthusiasm. There was still very little money, but one Sunday evening when Farahat arrived at the building site there was some news for him. Earlier in the day a man had driven up in a Mercedes and asked for Farahat. When he didn't find him, he left a message.

At that point, the work had ground almost to a halt, because they couldn't get cement for the upper storey of the church. Financing it was proving very difficult, and so was getting a licence. Farahat read the message and found it was brief and cryptic. It read, 'Samy Saad, Engineer, 14 Hassan El Akbar St. The appointment is for six in the evening.'

Farahat didn't have a clue who the man was. But he left right away to keep the appointment for six o'clock, and found the company in a central district of Cairo called Abdeen. He went in and found a secretary and some engineers in the office. He showed someone the piece of paper and they told him, 'Samy Saad is the owner of the company.'

Eagerly Farahat said, 'Oh – please take me to see him!'

As they got talking, Farahat soon realized that the owner of the company and the owner of the tractor bringing them water were one and the same. 'We are very grateful for the water, but now it's run out.'

It turned out that Samy had heard about Adham – how the tractor had crushed his head and how God had miraculously healed him when he was at death's door. This inspired Samy to offer Farahat more help. 'What exactly do you need?' he asked.

'What we really need is cement.'

'OK, take 10 tons of cement from Al-Haram, and whenever you need more we will send it until you have finished the church.'

So the miracle of Adham's healing had still further consequences. By amazing Samy, it had made it possible for the building work to go on. Through such miracles, God encouraged the labourers to forge ahead with their task. The new church, which covered an area of around 1,000 square metres, was now due to be finished in 1977.

Ordination

At this time the Patriarch made an announcement in the pages of *Al-Kiraza* magazine, the official bulletin of the Coptic Church. In it he said that he was going to ordain another man – not Farahat – as priest for the church of St Simaan the Tanner. Farahat, as the manager of *Al-Kiraza* Press, could not fail to notice the announcement. Given his strong sense of calling to this church's work, it is not hard to imagine his feelings.

Many *zeballeen* shared those feelings, for they formed a

delegation to make an appeal to the Patriarch. Everyone who had heard about the announcement went to him and said, 'Please, your holiness, all the people here know Brother Farahat. He is the one who has been with us since the beginning, sharing with us, working with us, and visiting us. He knows our homes and our lives and has always come back to us, even when we felt like giving it all up.'

The Patriarch paused to think. 'All right, I'll put this first ordination on hold and look into the situation again.'

The Patriarch is a firm believer in the principle that it is the people who should choose their priest. They won't accept an ordinand they don't know sent to them out of the blue. They must be convinced that the candidate *should* be ordained having seen the person at work during a period of practical service. So right from the beginning the candidate must be believed to be a true child of God. He must be living his ministry and getting to know the different kinds of service through being among the people.

This issue is never easy to settle. It takes prayer and tears, and in later years the church at Muqattam would agonize over future candidates for as long as four years before making their final choice. Even then, the ordinands were to travel at least three times a week, and in some cases every day, to the clerical college.

Finally, the Patriarch interviews the candidate and, if all goes well, ordains him. For Farahat, that day of decision was 15 January 1978. It was then that Pope Shenouda III 'in his love chose me – an ignorant *zabaal*'.

4 THE VOICE

Origins

Although Farahat was now Father Simaan, and ordained as priest of the church of St Simaan, he had few pretensions as to his education and training. On the contrary, he liked to emphasize that he came from a down-to-earth *fellaheen* or 'ploughman's' family, who lived in a tiny village.

The day Farahat was born there was a triple celebration. In the same family, there was a double wedding – and a new birth. In the traditional Egyptian countryside, the arrival of a baby boy is a very special occasion. (More so than if the baby is a girl, despite a long government campaign to convince people that 'a girl is like a boy'!) This boy was born on the same day (5 December 1941) that two uncles got married. So they called him 'Farahat', which means 'weddings'. Later he liked to think of his name as 'the Wedding to come', when Christ comes to take his bride, the Church.

The village where Farahat was born (which rejoices in the name of Meet Ayesh Kafr Yusuf Meet Ghamr Daqhaleya!) is near Al-Mansurah in the densely populated Nile Delta. Al-Mansurah is a provincial capital, situated on a broad sweep of a fast-flowing middle channel of the Delta. The furthest point reached by the Crusaders on several separate occasions, by 1941 it was under British administration. Surrounded by a richly fertile countryside, it was a fairly prosperous place to live, given the wartime conditions. But in terms of customs and traditions, the few kilometres that separated the city from the countryside represented a vast cultural gulf.

City and Country

Even today, city and countryside differ a great deal. In the city, numerous multinational companies like Macdonald's and Kentucky Fried Chicken clash incongruously with the history and rural position of the city, yet many indigenous shops are more glitzy. City-bred girls wear smart, somewhat Westernized clothes and go out in the evenings to the cinema and other such entertainments.

But even Egyptian city-dwellers would regard the opportunities of women and the free mixing between the sexes that is the norm in the Western world as excessive. They expect their daughters to go out in groups, often of the same sex, and to be home by a certain time. They don't allow 'dating' and a girl must not go out alone with a man until after a legal engagement ceremony that is just as public as a wedding. Their marriage is more a matter of two families getting together than two individuals. But in the city the young couple have their say in whom they marry and enjoy a certain measure of freedom. During the engagement they will get to know each other's personalities and lifestyles, and if they don't get on they can call the engagement off.

In the countryside in 1941, by contrast, it was still usual for people to get married because the elders of their village had decreed it in their childhood. Neither bride nor groom had any say in the matter: the word of the elders was enough. This traditional system could result in men and women leading somewhat separate lives even after marriage, and having rigidly defined roles. Even then there were tensions, and the frictions between the couple could be exacerbated because they had not chosen each other in the first place.

Gradually, a greater measure of choice came into being, to the point where today a man from the village could even choose to marry a girl from the city. However, if he does do this, culture-shock often results, as the girl frets at finding her freedom restricted, and being told she cannot go to this place or do certain things. She may long to go shopping as she used to, but the family may insist on sending someone to go for her. She may be frustrated by her new family and shock them by using make-up or dressing in Western fashions. She may even demand to go to places where men outside the family will see her – something that is not acceptable in the countryside.

Childhood and Youth

Farahat's father, Ibrahim, was a *fellah* (country farmer). He would have been as conservative as the next man in the village, but he was also a committed Coptic Christian and, along with his wife, Maryam, built up a Christian family life. Therefore one place he did allow Farahat's mother to go was the local church of the Virgin Mary. Farahat was the youngest of her six children and she always took him to church with her. When he was only six years old she took him to see the bishop of the diocese of Daqheleyya, who agreed to ordain Farahat as a *shamaas* (deacon). In theory, the minimum age for becoming a deacon was twenty-five, but the rule was simply not observed. In the early days of the Egyptian Church the deacon would have performed similar duties to an Anglican deacon today, but now their main role was to chant parts of the service, usually in groups. The archdeacon was a kind of master of ceremonies for the service. So in effect Farahat was joining the choir – he was not going to preach at the age of six!

Maryam always made sure Farahat went to Sunday school, and this had a very big influence on him. He especially remembers a *khaadim* (lay-worker) coming from Cairo to speak to them. The story this man told moved Farahat to tears. We don't know what he said, but a typical example of the kind of testimonies circulating in Sunday schools about that time is that of Lilian Trasher. Lilian came to Egypt without any resources or any plan save that she had a deep conviction that God had led her there, and would show her what her ministry was to be. It turned out to be looking after orphans in the countryside of Upper Egypt – and there were many instances when she was forced to rely completely on God to provide for them. On one occasion she had run out of food, but she told the orphans that Jesus would provide for their needs. She had no idea how.

The time for the meal arrived and in faith she got all the orphans to sit down in front of their empty plates. They said grace in the usual way. She assured them Jesus would provide, and there came a knock on the door. A van had run out of petrol outside. These were the war years of the 1940s when fuel was rationed, and there was no way the van was going to complete the journey before the food inside it went off. The owner offered the food to Lilian and the orphans had far more to eat than they normally would!

Hearing of God acting in real life changed Farahat's whole outlook. It wasn't long before his friends noticed this, and were eager to listen to his ideas. Even though at this stage he had no first-hand experience of God acting in his life, there was plenty of opportunity for the influence of Sunday school to take root in Farahat – for it wasn't until he was eleven that he was sent to a government-run school.

Reckoning with God

It was after this change of school that peer-group pressure started to come into play in a big way. More and more, Farahat found himself following his new friends and began to drift away from his Christian beliefs and lifestyle. By the age of sixteen he had drifted away from the Church completely, and just when it seemed that he was crashing out of the Christian life completely, God caught him. One day he was in his room studying when a voice from nowhere demanded, 'What's this latest sin you've committed? Where you're heading is hell.'

'What's all this about sin and hell?' protested Farahat. 'I'm far better behaved and more moral than most people of my age.'

But then suddenly he saw himself in a picture projected on to the wall in front of him. It was as if God was running a complete cine-film of his life. 'These are all the things you have done, from when you first knew sin up to this moment,' said the voice within.

Despite his protestations, Farahat already felt weighed down by sin, and at times it really frightened him. If anyone mentioned death, or if he heard of someone dying, he couldn't sleep a wink for several nights running. So when the voice said, 'What's this latest sin you've committed? Where you're heading is hell,' despair overwhelmed him. Casting around for any means of support, he grabbed hold of a book in front of him. It belonged to his sister, and he'd never even opened it before. The title was *Prayers of the Saints*.

The first thing he read really hit him between the eyes. People, it said, 'are heartless and cruel and never do right' (Psalms 14.1). 'No one is acceptable to God!' (Romans 3.10) was the verdict. We are 'less than a puff of air' (Psalms 62.9). The confession 'I have sinned and done wrong since the day I was born' (Psalms 51.5) seemed to Farahat to sum up the 'cine-film' of his life. The complaint 'something in me keeps me from doing what I know is right' (Romans 7.21b) reminded him of all his past struggles with sin. 'What a miserable person I am' (Romans 7.24) was a fair summary of how he felt.

After that, the tone of the verses in the book changed. 'But to all who received him, who believed in his name, he gave power to become children of God' (John 1.12 *RSV*). Instead of despair, there was hope: 'everyone that the Father has given me will come to me, and I won't turn any of them away' (John 6.37). Christ could make him clean: 'the blood of his Son Jesus washes all our sins away' (1 John 1.7b).

Suddenly Farahat sensed just how much he'd sinned, saw that the love of Christ could reach him, but felt powerless to do anything about it. He'd no idea how to turn his understanding of the words into effective prayer. But turning to the next page he found just the words that he needed.

It said, 'Lord, I have burdened you and cheated you by my evil deeds. I was the one who moved away from you. You know all my secrets and all my life, but I am coming to you now. Forgive me, give me a new heart and purify me with your blood. "Create in me a clean heart, O God, and put a new and right spirit within me" (Psalms 51.10 *RSV*).

I make a covenant by your grace that I will not backslide again, since your power is in your weakness and I am very weak.'

When Farahat had finished praying he felt a great weight lift from his shoulders. For the first time ever, he picked up the Bible and read it not because it was a deacon's duty, but because he really wanted to know what was in it. Amazingly, it fell open in John's Gospel at the same verse that he'd read in *Prayers of the Saints*: 'To all who received him, who believed in his name, he gave power to become children of God' (John 1.12 *RSV*). This confirmed to Farahat that God had really spoken to him, that he had now received God into his inmost being, and begun a new life with him.

About midnight he fell asleep and dreamt he was wearing a white *galibeyya* (a long tunic). It looked very smart, but there was a black spot over his heart. He heard a voice say, 'Why are you wearing that? The black mark looks very bad.'

The dream continued with a hawker in the street outside calling out that he was carrying white paint. Farahat thought he would go down and buy the paint and use it to get rid of the black mark. So he opened up the door of the room (which was part of a very big house) and went out. He then saw a man in white who looked wonderful. With him was a lady, who was also wearing white. As he got nearer to the man, he realized he was radiating a pure and almost blinding beauty. Farahat found that the sheer force of this beauty kept him from approaching the man. But the man said to Farahat, 'Come, my son, what is it you want?' and lifted him on to his shoulders.

Farahat told him, 'I want to buy some white paint from that hawker.'

'Why?'

'Because I have a black mark I want to get rid of – my *galibeyya* looks terrible.'

'Fine, but I don't sell.'

Farahat was taken aback. He needed the paint, but felt he could hardly say, 'Well, give it to me for nothing then!' Farahat realized that this dream was an encounter with God. Here was someone who wouldn't sell, and Farahat wanted to buy, so he fell silent. Finally the man said, 'All right, I will wipe it away for you – but on one condition.'

'What's that?' Farahat asked.

'Don't get it dirty again.'

Farahat agreed. The man stretched out his hand and touched the black mark. Looking down at his chest, Farahat saw the mark transform itself into a spot that was whiter than the white of his tunic.

After that, Farahat fell into a deep sleep, only to have another dream. This time he found a fish on his right hand. A very beautiful white dove came and sat in the same place as the fish – and this scene was replayed in the dream three nights running. Farahat was a bit puzzled by the dream, then put it to the back of his mind.

Transformation

Some time after this Farahat stunned his mother Maryam by agreeing to do exactly what she asked without arguing. This was *so* unheard of that when he did it again and again she got seriously worried about his state of mind! 'What's come over you?' she demanded anxiously, suddenly preferring the awkward son she was used to!

So Farahat told her about the voices and the dreams. Maryam had had a very limited education, but Farahat sensed that God had given her 'very great grace'. She never missed a communion service, and at five o'clock every morning was on her knees in prayer. Her love for God was expressed in her love for her neighbours. She prayed for all the Christians one by one, and many Muslims would tell her their problems and also ask her to pray for them.

When Farahat told his mother what had happened, she said, 'My son, the person you met was Christ and the Virgin was with him. He stretched out his pierced hand to wipe away the sin in your heart. This means that you now have a new heart.' The dove, of course, was the Holy Spirit. 'The fish,' she said, 'is a sign that God will give you souls as a result of your turning back to him and living in him.'

This was the beginning of Farahat's life in Christ, but lots of changes were still to follow. At the time he was nearly seventeen and was hooked on popular, romantic love songs. He even had a book of them. This was the summer of 1958 and as usual Farahat was spending his school holidays on his father's farm. He loved to go out and watch the workers in the fields and, as he sat astride a donkey, would sing these love songs to himself.

One morning, though, he woke up to find a voice saying to him, 'No, don't sing those words any more. Now you're going to praise and sing hymns to me.' Straight away and without being fully aware of what he was doing, Farahat got up, found the book of love songs and burnt it. Never again did Farahat revert to singing these songs.

Sometimes when he met his friends he began to swear and lie in the way he had been used to doing. But this time, God's voice brought him up short. 'No, you're not going to swear and curse any more – you're going to bless.' And whenever Farahat did misuse his tongue, God immediately stopped him.

When he tried to go to the places he used to haunt before coming to the Lord, God turned him back. 'No, your legs are going to carry you to my house,' a voice within seemed to be saying.

Village Outreach

Despite the need to learn new ways, Farahat found he loved going to church and serving the Lord. He longed to preach in the church and reached the point where he said to his father, 'I really want to go out and preach.'

'The *omda* (village headman) reads out the sermon in the church,' said his father. 'Who are you to go there and preach?'

'No, I must go out and preach,' Farahat persisted.

'But you are still a young boy – you must be out of your mind to think you can preach. Be sensible and don't talk such nonsense,' came the put-down.

But Farahat had a restlessness within him and a fire in his heart that convinced him he *must* go and preach in the church and tell people about Christ. Yet no one ever *preached* in the village church, because the person who acted as priest there was a monk who did not preach. Instead, the *omda* simply stood up and read from a book of sermons.

So for the time being, Farahat started where he could – by speaking to his friends who could see that his life had been transformed. In this time of his first encounter with Christ, of repentance, Farahat began to read the Bible, pray and serve in the church. He worked very hard at this time, first in Ismailiyya, where he stayed with his brother, and then in Cairo.

But even while living in Cairo Farahat felt extremely

concerned about the village he was born in, since he knew just how needy it was. So he loved returning to the village with some friends, who like him were Christian lay-workers. Every Sunday they used to get up at six o'clock in the morning to go to the village. They went to mass at the village church and preached there – then out to the surrounding villages, which didn't have any churches at all. They went round the houses, knocking on doors and talking to the people about Christ. Then they took them to a meeting. They also took some children to Sunday school. On such days Farahat would not get home again until midnight. This ministry made as great an impact on his life as it did on those they ministered to.

It was during this time, in 1964, that Farahat was working on the newspaper called *Al-Gumhurriya* (*The Republic*). He had a Christian colleague there called Fahmi Arryan whom he used to talk with about Christ. One day Fahmi said to him, 'You talk to me one-to-one, but why don't you come and see what it's like in our area. It's near to Cairo, but the Coptic children know nothing about Jesus. They get newspapers and spread them out like prayer-mats, just like the Muslims do. Come and speak about Christ.'

Deliverance in the City

Farahat agreed and then spent some time praying to see if God really did want him to serve in that area. It was a satellite town just to the north of Cairo. Eventually he began a ministry there and his partner in this work for some years was Engineer Maqyas Hanna. Together they ran a Sunday school, meetings for young men and women (held separately), and open (all-age, mixed) meetings. And God was glorified through it all.

This was the first place that God did a miracle through Farahat's ministry. By this time he was engaged to Su'aad, and she was with him. One day they encountered someone who clearly was being affected by evil spirits. Farahat had no idea about praying for the sick, exorcism, etc., but he heard God saying to him, 'Pray'. So that was what he did. He was very thankful and relieved to find that the Lord exerted his authority through him and the evil spirit left.

This kind of deliverance from demon possession became an ordinary, regular feature of Farahat's work. To the Western mind, this is something spectacular, out of the ordinary, and to the rationalist is a matter for great controversy. Even in the East it is a sensitive issue, and the Coptic Patriarch has decreed that exorcism should not take place in public worship, but only in private. Yet the problem of demon oppression is for many non-Christians part of everyday life. They sense the presence of 'powers' and 'beings'. The things they see around them may change from one state to another, and the way they see reality is in some ways much more like that of biblical times than the average Western Christian's view.[1]

This world was not strange to Farahat; he regularly encountered it. He was, if anything, much more excited and challenged to be asked to do what many Western lay people take for granted – to preach in a public meeting. This was in the same area (on the extreme northern edge of Cairo) where the exorcism took place. It seemed that they had only been going there a very short time when Farahat's partner in ministry, Engineer Maqyas, said to him, '*You'll* be taking the next service.'

This invitation – or command – drove Farahat to his knees. He'd never got involved in evangelism or preaching so close to the city. He could do such things in villages, but

Cairo was a different matter. There he had served by listening to people and following them up. He had taught in Sunday school, but never taken a public meeting.

In asking God for guidance about what to say, for the first time Farahat had the experience of receiving a word to give to others. The simple message was 'God is love' – 'God so loved the world that he gave his only son, that whoever believes in him would not perish but have eternal life' (John 3.16). Encouraged by what God seemed to be asking him to say, Farahat took the plunge and found himself speaking for about an hour and a quarter.

Su'aad

This particular service was the start of a ministry for Farahat in that area that lasted several years. Apart from Maqyas, Farahat's main encourager was his fiancée, Su'aad. From the very beginning of their engagement she got fully involved, sharing with Farahat both in prayer and ministry.

They plunged enthusiastically into this work even though there was plenty for Farahat to do at the newspaper. In 1967, *The Republic* had many shattering events to report. In June, President Nasir broadcast his resignation after Israeli planes had destroyed much of the Egyptian air force on the ground. The Israeli army had taken over the Sinai peninsula. Almost the whole population of Egypt demonstrated in support of Nasir and a war of attrition began, with all that that meant in terms of economic sacrifice.

It was during this period that Farahat and Su'aad got married. And whatever their material circumstances, they kept their minds and hearts focused on service. Su'aad took responsibility for teenage girls and young women at a church in a place called Al-Hafzeya. She also accompanied

Farahat to the area he ministered in. What started out as a few meetings and a Sunday school grew into a big congregation now known as the Church of the Virgin. From small beginnings, God was using their commitment and faith to achieve greater and greater things.

5 STONES OR SOULS?

Family Life

Within a few years of their first visits to the rubbish collectors, and certainly before Farahat could be ordained in 1978, he and Su'aad had to come to a decision about where they were going to live: would they continue to visit the area from Shubra, or would they make the rubbish collectors' community *their* community?

As a lay-worker, it had been all right for Farahat to visit the rubbish collectors from his place of work and from his home in Shubra. But it was unthinkable for a Coptic priest not to live in his parish. By being ordained Farahat committed himself and his family to living not only *for* the rubbish collectors, but also *with* them.

So when Farahat and Su'aad came to serve the rubbish collectors, they set aside even their modest middle-class status. They wanted to become like the people they had come to serve, so that they would like and accept them. This caused the couple some serious heart-searching as they moved with their two small children into a violent neighbourhood teeming with pigs and rubbish. By now they had a boy and a girl, Albeer and Mary. Just by visiting other mothers Su'aad could bring lice home to her children, and there was always the danger of their catching hepatitis, tetanus or meningitis.

All *zeballeen* mothers faced the same problems as Su'aad. One, called Samia, found God helped her through all the heartbreaking experiences of her life. Married at fourteen, the year before Farahat and Su'aad first visited the area, she was to lose four children through accidents and childhood diseases. Her husband and mother-in-law wanted her to have more children to help collect and sort rubbish, and she was to have five children still living by the time she was thirty-seven. Her eldest son got married and lived with his family in one of the two small rooms in their dwelling. As a hard-pressed mother and grandmother, she has a very difficult life, yet she says, 'Jesus makes everything seem different.' He is her friend and she can count on him when things get tough.

Ministry

Once he took on the ordination name of Father Simaan, Farahat aimed to be like his namesake. The Simaan of old got up early to take water to housebound people before he started his day's work, so trying to be like Simaan meant Farahat serving the poor and vulnerable. So the new Father Simaan got alongside the rubbish collectors as any other rubbish collector would.

Since the rubbish collectors couldn't possibly understand theological terms, Father Simaan didn't use them. Standing up before them, he became just like them – knowing nothing. He spurned any professional priestly technique in his preaching to them, and fifteen minutes beforehand he didn't know what he would say. The countdown continued – ten minutes, five – still he didn't know! All he had were a few disconnected ideas. But once he got started God took over and his whole talk fell into place.

Father Simaan didn't have an agenda in his preaching. It wasn't him they came to hear, so he'd wait for Christ to speak. No technique could satisfy the kaleidoscope of needs that faced him, and not all who came were *zeballeen*. People from a wide range of social backgrounds met to pray. Some wept, some pulled their hair, others shouted aloud. Whatever they did, Father Simaan accepted it. It was the Holy Spirit moving them, not him.

Preaching wasn't his priority so much as proving Jesus' teaching. Jesus' disciples spent time with him before he sent them out to preach, and by sharing his life he met their need. By this stage, Father Simaan had a team of lay-workers and he wanted them to be able to see Jesus in each other. Only then could they demonstrate his life to others. The most important thing the team could do was to invite Jesus into their lives – and *then* invite the *zeballeen*.

Support Network

Father Simaan knew what it was like to be a lay-worker, and he certainly didn't believe in workers being loners. Even at the start of his ministry he had always linked up with another brother. He would work and the other would pray, or he would pray and his partner would speak. 'Two are a mirror to each other and take care of each other. That is why Jesus sent his disciples out two by two,' he would say.

Father Simaan's first prayer-partner never appeared in public. Yet he was always there for him – silent, but sensitive to the leading of the Spirit. They served God together, but this friend took no action unless Father Simaan specifically asked him to. Eventually a third prayer-partner joined them, and then a fourth. And so the inner core of the team formed and grew.

Although the committed core was small, this reflected Father Simaan's care to lay firm foundations for the work. They began with a small team, because he wanted everyone who took part in evangelism to know Christ personally. The most lowly servant in the church had to know that God was changing him and had given his life a radically new direction. If the church let people serve on the basis of their natural abilities rather than following Christ's leading, then the work might begin with a bang, but sooner or later it would fizzle out. Far better for the work to begin in a small and quiet way, but grow later.

Festival of St Simaan

Small and quiet the work may have been, but the Patriarch, Pope Shenouda, took a personal interest in the early efforts of his new priest. Thus Father Simaan went to see Pope Shenouda in his monastery of Anba Rweiss to invite him for the festival of St Simaan the Tanner. Late in November 1978 the community lined his route, waving palm branches and chanting their welcome. People released doves as the Patriarch passed by, after which he celebrated communion in the church. His visit greatly encouraged the people and he repeated it on the same occasion the following November.

Gradually the festival of St Simaan grew in importance in the eyes of the people. The reason for celebrating it in November was simple. Back in the tenth century, it was November when Patriarch Abraam had called the Church to fast and pray for three days before the miracle that split the mountain, so the Patriarch decided that the Copts should fast each year in memory of it.

The Coptic Church observes many fasts during the year. The longest is the Christmas fast. In Patriarch Abraam's time, it lasted forty days. If it had been a matter of choosing any time of year, the Church could have found one when fasts were shorter. Yet it was to this fast that they decided to add three days in memory of the mountain moving. Since they celebrated the new fast 25 to 27 November, this tells us that the original fast began on 25 November and the miracle itself took place on the third day, 27 November AD 979.[1]

The twentieth-century Father Simaan believed he was building his mission on the foundation that the tenth-century Simaan had laid. His fascination for the mountain and the area around it was so strong he felt like 'a fish out of water' outside it. He felt that he could not be effective if he strayed beyond the borders of that historical place where he belonged. By confining himself to the people of this area, he felt he could make more impact for the gospel; and the more he moved around the community, the more his roles multiplied. God was adding to his gifts, so not only could he preach, but he could also offer a healing ministry. Last but not least, he grew in leadership ability, so that he was also effective as an administrator.

Dealing with Deprivation

This gift for leadership was a key asset in facing the challenges presented by the area. A World Bank report of July 1978 counted 15,000 people in Manshiyat Nasir, all living in the most deprived conditions to be found anywhere in Cairo. And despite disease and a high death rate, their number was to double in eighteen years. A programme for progressive development of the area began in 1980 on the initiative of the Cairo governorate and the World Bank. This involved organizing the rubbish collecting and recycling services into a comprehensive system that could cover the entire city. In less than ten years, the *zeballeen* were to turn their area into the main centre for recycling rubbish.

This was good, but it only tackled the material causes of deprivation. There was only one registered organization that had some link to the Church. Anba Samweel, the Coptic Bishop of Social Services, had started an organization that was run by the *zeballeen* themselves for their social improvement. And despite the connection with the Church, Anba Samweel managed to legitimate the group's activities by setting it up as a Society of Rubbish Collectors.[2]

The date of the Society's registration, 23 January 1974, shows that it was the first to experiment with 'development' work locally. At first it drew its members from the heads of prominent families in Muqattam, as Anba Samweel was keenly aware of their influence on the rubbish collectors. But sadly, his personal contribution ended on 6 October 1981 when he was caught up in a hail of bullets that Muslim extremists were aiming at President Sadat and his entourage. Thus the assassination of President Sadat resulted in the martyrdom of Samweel, a faithful servant of the Coptic Church.

The society that Anba Samweel founded continued its work under a different name. But neither government agencies, nor foreign funding organizations, even when they worked with local people, could deal with the spiritual roots of economic deprivation and its social consequences. They could not see, as Father Simaan did, that the residents' greatest hope lay in preserving the rich spiritual heritage of the site itself.

Eventually the day came when an influential person in government wanted to move the people out of their houses and off their land. No doubt he viewed their way of life as backward and their housing as a health hazard, as it mixed people together with animals. But Father Simaan felt passionately that if the *zeballeen* had to move again, this would pull them apart. It would uproot them from the bedrock of their mountain and break up their community of faith. Both Church and State would be the losers. So Father Simaan decided to appeal to the compassionate heart of the Patriarch and tell him the whole story: 'His holiness answered me in faith, "God who moved the mountain of Muqattam by faith . . . will remove the thoughts of these people [in authority] from them."'[3]

Events proved the Patriarch right in his unwavering faith. The authorities abandoned their plan and Father Simaan made good his conviction that Manshiyat Nasir was the right place for the people to be, and the work of the church continued.

From the 1980s onwards, Father Simaan organized home visiting and follow-up services to the *zeballeen* district and the surrounding areas, such as Ezbit Bakheet and Doweeqa. He did this through lay-workers consecrated to the task. But it was not until the end of the decade that the Patriarch ordained other priests to share in this ministry.

Visiting and Follow-up

Between 1978 and 1985 the lay team was hard at work visiting people and following them up. Their ministry was 99 per cent practical work and only 1 per cent talk. If they were going to cover the whole district they could go into only one home in each street. Here they might find anything from twenty to fifty people. More would then come in from the street, until a group of up to one hundred would be gathered. Each street would have a separate session with Father Simaan.

Father Simaan organized the lay-workers in a straight-forward way, according to their gifts. No one person was expected to do everything: 'Some sang, some prayed, some followed people up, some served, some ministered in the communion service with me as deacons – it was a shared ministry, everything was shared . . .' Drawing on his own experience as a lay-worker, Father Simaan helped those serving with him to set themselves targets in their personal work. Often this was difficult: it meant sticking at a task through thick and thin.

Anyone who truly turned to Christ could become a lay-worker, but first they had to be discipled by others who had been tried and tested. They needed to share the lives of these workers so that they could worship and grow, until they reached the point when they could lead lives of ministry. The problem was getting young disciples to spend long enough with the lay-workers to grow effectively.

One non-*zeballeen* lay-worker who joined the team describes how Father Simaan asked him to concentrate on three older men in the church. They had come back to their faith, but were 'still wobbling'. He tried to make friends with these three and spent time reading the Bible with one of them, but the other two were always 'too busy'. It was easier to win their friendship than their commitment. They were ready enough to chat affably with their friend, but not to spend time reading the Bible or praying with him. Father Simaan helped his lay-worker to tackle the problem, in a way that convinced him that 'if you're going to be effective, you've got to focus on a few people, you've got to stay in one place, you've got to concentrate on one thing'. It was this understanding that encouraged a worker to stick to the task, however long it took.

Part of the problem with persuading *zeballeen* to keep up their Christian commitment was the amount of time they spent working just to stay alive. It took great discipline for them to go to a discipleship meeting after a tiring day. Yet if they didn't keep going to the meetings, then illiteracy or a very limited reading ability would stop them from feeding themselves spiritually from the Bible. Consequently, many 'fell away'.

However, Father Simaan didn't let his lay-workers dwell on such setbacks. Instead he made the most of the encouragements that came their way. If someone did turn to the Lord, Father Simaan would organize a big celebration. This was called a 'repentance party'. Since the government system of identity cards in Egypt fixes your religion from birth, you don't say someone has 'become a Christian'. Instead you say they have 'come back to our Lord' or 'repented'. When someone repented Father Simaan would always have a brace of pigs killed and throw a party. The whole church could come to a sizzling barbecue on the rooftop of the convert's house. They would put chairs up on the roof and have a resounding time of praise and worship. People could get carried away and the flood of praise would go on well into the night.

If Father Simaan's penchant for roast pork was a predictable source of refreshment for his lay-workers, his quest for new ideas always kept them guessing as to what was coming next. New projects came off the drawing-board thick and fast. Soon there were workshops for carpentry and electrical skills, and later two bookshops. The Muqattam area offered much scope for experimentation. From time to time a breeze-block-type structure would appear, only to be torn down again quite quickly to make way for a better building. Father Simaan needed a good deal of imagination and faith to keep trying until his building projects really fitted the needs of mission in Muqattam.

Ministry on the Mountain

Much effort went into drawing out the potential of the mountain as a base for ministry. On a flat, rocky shelf halfway up the mountain the team planned to add a retreat centre for training the lay-workers. They called it the *deir* (monastery), although there were no monks. It included buildings for auxiliary ministries as well as churches.

The first site on the mountain to be used without interruption as a place of worship was a converted cave. Worshippers sat in a bank reaching up to the cave's mouth. When it opened in 1986 it was small and its facilities very basic. Yet the site had the potential to be greatly enlarged. They called it 'the cavern'. Plunging into the cavern to do his share of the building work was for Father Simaan a welcome opportunity of being incognito for a while. Once he'd been at it for a short time the black dust of the mountain covered him so thickly that it was extremely hard to recognize him. Since he wore a long black *galibeyya* and black cap, you often couldn't make out his face from his clothes!

Yet even those who did recognize him didn't necessarily recognize the value of what he was doing. Sincere believers would come up to him and say, 'Are you serving the stones?' Some people close to him rebuked him for not spending more time in personal work. 'Do stones matter more than souls?' was their question. Father Simaan gave no glib answers. He hardly understood better than they did why God wanted them to do all this construction work. All he knew was that there was a vision driving him on that God was going to fulfil. What the outcome would be, he didn't know. What mattered was that God was leading him.

It was hard to fathom the need for so much construction

work partly because it was so difficult to persuade people to come and use the *existing* church facilities. At that time, the main public meeting was on Tuesdays. Lay-workers would meet for prayer and then go round the streets in pairs, inviting people to come. Most people they met said, 'Oh yes, I'm coming, I'm coming' – and then didn't. Egyptian culture does not encourage directly refusing a request, and so words are not necessarily an indication of intention. It was like the parable of the son who says to his father, 'Yes, I'm going to the vineyard', but doesn't go (Matthew 21.30).

The Committed Core

Time spent inviting people to meetings could be better used talking with people one-to-one or doing group training sessions. Much seed fell on thorns or thistles, or shallow ground that produced no lasting fruit. Yet a committed core began to emerge, of people who really caught the vision for the gospel and for going forward in Christian service. Young men worked at their jobs during the day and engaged in ministry of one kind or another in the evenings. Teenage girls got involved in teaching, and some kept their vision for prayer and witness after getting married and having children.

Some examples will show what a commitment this demanded.

Suma was from a poor family that lived at ground level with their pigs and their rubbish. The family didn't get on with one another well. Unlike other families who tried to better themselves, they never built a second storey on to their house to lift themselves above the filth. The only way Suma could raise her expectations was to attend the church school as a teenager. There was a church meeting on Thursdays that Suma could go to, but by the time she was sixteen she was engaged to a man she hardly knew. When they got married a year later, it was clear that her husband was not a believer.

But the couple did have one advantage, not often found in the affluent West. Suma and her husband both believed that since they were married, they should stick together and learn to love each other. When problems arose, they didn't give up. Suma knew a teacher at the church school from a more privileged family whose husband encouraged her to work. Suma and her husband went to this Christian couple for counselling – and Suma's husband came to faith. Eventually Suma became a self-confident teacher at the church school where she had studied as a teenager.

The teenage girls had their church meeting on Thursdays. The government employees who had to work on Sundays could go to a communion service on Friday mornings. This was held in the Church of St Simaan below the mountain, the one built after the miraculous healing of Adham's head. One evening in the week the committed core of lay-workers met – and wept over their sins and unworthiness to pray. Some of them used to go away by themselves into a corner of the room and cry out aloud and at length, while other people were praying. This was confusing for a visitor, but no one doubted they were praying in earnest.

Rediscoveries

For six long years they prayed that God would show them how to discover the entrance to a new meeting place. Then in 1986 a workman who was lifting a rock dropped it and it crashed down to the level below. When the dust cleared they could see that the impact had opened up a previously invisible underground cavity. When their eyes had finally adjusted to the gloom, the workers found beneath their feet 'a starkly beautiful cave with natural rock pillars'.[4]

The cave's presence was a constant reminder that God could have more surprises in store for them yet. By 1990, they had started work on fashioning a church out of the cave. To their surprise, the natural shape of the cave fitted perfectly the outline of a traditional Coptic church. It divided naturally into three sections: for enquirers, the baptized and the communicants. All they had to do was hang a curtain in front of the space that would typically serve as a sanctuary.

The place may have been a church or at least a meeting place long ago, before falling into disuse and getting filled with rubble. Traces found among the rubbish suggested that there had been a rail for tying horses. Organic remains suggested food and accessories used in Napoleon's army. He had invaded Egypt in 1798, and for three years confronted the country with the full range of Western technology. The West was also given an insight into Egypt by the work of eminent professors that Napoleon took with him on his campaign. Eventually Nelson sunk the French fleet and the British helped the Ottoman Turks to expel Napoleon's army by September 1801.[5]

Whatever it had been used for before, the cave was reopened in 1991 as a church. It was named after Anba Boula, a hermit monk who followed the pattern of St Anthony.

Long ago, in response to falling standards of Christian life in the cities, Egyptian Christians pioneered a counter-culture by staying single and living a simple lifestyle. At first they tried this in local churches, but increasingly they followed the example of St Anthony, who in 270 sold his estates and went to live in the desert.

Egypt lends itself to such withdrawal because 97 per cent of the land is desert. Towns were limited mainly to the narrow strip of the Nile valley in the south, or to the fertile region of the Nile river delta in the north. In the northern desert St Anthony lived as a hermit and his disciples followed a solitary way of life; in the southern desert St Pachomius set a pattern of large communities which had made a radical break from society. In between the two regions and the two models, were the monks of Nitria who lived in small groups near a spiritual father and met for worship at weekends.[6]

Such lifestyles attracted a lot of interest in the West. Monks with Egyptian names reached Ireland and stayed there till their deaths. They may have been the inspiration for St Patrick, who set the pattern of small communities as bases from which Celtic monks could reach Britain with the gospel.

Although it has no monks, Coptic visitors call the Muqattam Mountain retreat centre site 'the monastery'. So for them the cave church named after Anba Boula conjured up images of the ascetic spiritual lifestyle of the desert. There was space in the church for 400 worshippers. When they entered it one morning they were shocked to find all the cave walls blackened. It seems there had been a fire the night before, yet the smoke had left untouched the altar curtains and an icon of Christ.[7] The believers wondered why God would allow such damage to the church, but later came to see the incident as providential.

Egypt is still, nominally at least, following certain aspects of nineteenth-century Ottoman Turkish law that aimed to restrict church building, repairs and activities. It is very hard to get permission to build a new church and there are far fewer church buildings in Egypt than the Copts need. In this instance, a delegation came to find out what the Copts were doing 'building' a church on government land. If they received no satisfactory explanation, they could close it down immediately. But the blackened nature of the interior persuaded the delegation that the church wasn't new. A typical feature of ancient Coptic buildings is a blackened ceiling and walls darkened with smoke from candles used by worshippers down the ages. Thus the Department of Antiquities decided that the church had existed for centuries and they gave it protected status.

Three years after the discovery of Anba Boula in 1986 came another remarkable confirmation that God was watching over the efforts on the mountain. In 1989 workers on the cliff-face dislodged a large boulder and sent it crashing down into a courtyard some 30 metres below. Many people lived in the buildings around it, and plenty of pigs in it, yet no one was hurt – neither human nor animal.[8]

6 _MIRACLES_

Finding the Saint

At the beginning of 1989 God had laid it on the heart of Father Simaan to look for the body of St Simaan the Tanner. His whereabouts at the time of the miracle of moving the Muqattam Mountain in the tenth century were a mystery. After the miracle, the people drifted back to their homes, and it would have been true to Simaan's self-effacing character if he had melted into the crowd. Patriarch Abraam himself was unable to find him and a rumour spread that he had thrown himself under the mountain, to escape worldly adulation.

Yet this was highly unlikely, since only the Patriarch knew of St Simaan's role on the day of the miracle and promised to keep it a secret until after St Simaan's death. In fact, Patriarch Abraam himself died the same year that the miracle took place, in 979. Eventually Father Simaan discovered that the Copts had buried the tenth patriarch, Yo'annas, next to St Simaan in the cemetery of Al-Habash in Old Cairo.[1] They did the same with Patriarch Gabriel in 1378.

That meant that Father Simaan could narrow down the site of the burial to a specific part of Old Cairo. Specialists who were working on restoring St Mary's Church, in the correct area for the cemetery, then discovered a skeleton 1 metre below the southern wall. The bones evidently belonged to a person small of stature, with a head balding in front. It seems likely that the skeleton is that of St Simaan as it bears a great similarity to an icon found in the Hanging Church that shows St Simaan and Patriarch Abraam together.

Buried near the skeleton the restorers found a clay pot that was over one thousand years old. This supports the dating of the skeleton. On 11 July 1992, the Copts celebrated the life of St Simaan the Tanner in Muqattam. That day, they brought some of his mortal remains in solemn procession to the church that bears his name. They installed the clay pot in the same compartment where they laid their saint's remains to rest.

The return of the body of the one who prayed to move the mountain to the people of the mountain, proved to be a potent symbol of faith. Visitors to Muqattam dared to hope that God would work as powerfully in their time as he had done in St Simaan's.

Signs and Wonders

Many people would kiss the glass case where St Simaan's bones lay, wrapped in their cylinder of velvet. Clearly they hoped for some special blessing. Yet today's Father Simaan sees signs and miracles as given by God for his purposes, not to satisfy the whims of the human will. 'Not by might, nor by power, but by my Spirit, says the LORD of hosts' (Zechariah 4.6). When God acts in power, the greatest miracle he can do is to win the soul back to Christ. Healing or raising the sick is a sign to encourage the ministry of believers. 'Whoever believes in me, will do the things that I am doing, and even greater things' (John 14.12).

Building on the promises of God, Father Simaan and his team asked God to fulfil them. The secret was prayer; for it was faith that had moved that mountain. For this very reason they lived on that mountain, the mountain of prayer and faith, expecting to experience miracles. Just as Christ moved the mountain in the past, so he could move powerfully in the present: 'Jesus Christ is the same, yesterday, today and forever' (Hebrews 13.8).

One example of this was Sobhy, a building worker who experienced both the miracle of grace, and the miracle of healing. He repented and turned to Christ after listening to a cassette tape from the Muqattam ministry. Tears came to his eyes and God began to deal with him. After being drawn to follow Christ, in 1991 Sobhy found the opportunity to serve him by working on a church on the mountain.

Sobhy takes up the story: 'One day I went up on the scaffolding to put into position a triangular-shaped stone. I did this and then the concrete surround gave way, shaking the scaffolding I was standing on from top to bottom. I fell off, and as I was falling I completely lost consciousness.'

They rushed Sobhy to hospital in Heliopolis, with blood flowing out of his mouth and nose. The first X-rays showed that he had a fracture of the skull, complicated by an extradural haematoma. This is a blood clot between the coverings (meninges) of the brain and the skull. There were also signs of increased pressure on the brain (intra-cranial tension), such as vomiting and continued loss of consciousness. A neurological specialist who saw Sobhy recommended an operation to evacuate the blood clot. Without the operation, he would die of pressure on the brain.

Sobhy commented: 'There was going to be a dangerous life-or-death operation. *Abuna* [Father Simaan] prayed for me for three hours until my breath came back into my lungs.'[2]

After praying for Sobhy, Father Simaan felt God was saying, 'I will cure him'. Sobhy would not need an operation after all. Tests run on the second day could find no more signs of pressure increasing on the brain. Further X-rays showed that the brain was free of the blood clot and that the fracture in the skull had healed. Sobhy is now in excellent health and enjoying life to the full.

Another miracle followed an accident involving a girl hit by a huge stone. An orthopaedic doctor saw the X-ray, which showed damage to the second and third vertebrae of the spine. He recommended an operation and the parents decided to go ahead with it. When it was all over the surgeon told them that their daughter was paraplegic. She couldn't move her legs and was doubly incontinent.

The distraught parents brought the girl to Father Simaan for prayer. She can now move about and is no longer incontinent. Her spine, which had been badly bent by the impact of the rock, is now perfectly straight.

In 1991–2 the work-force turned their attention to a chamber right inside the original cavern, which had about 140,000 tons of rock in it. This project received some help from Tear Fund in England in addition to local support. Out of the rock took shape the conference hall of St Mark, which can hold 2,000 people. Just to one side of it was a space which Father Simaan began to use as his prayer room. He prefers it to the original hole under the rock that is no longer private enough, being near the entrance to the site of the retreat centre.

While this project was going on, a man called Magdy came to work at the retreat centre building site on Muqattam. On his very first day they assigned him to work on building a fountain. To do this he had to move blocks of stone from high up the mountain down to the bottom.

Not knowing his way around, he put his foot in the wrong place and fell from the cliff above the retreat centre, a drop of 13 or 14 metres.

Father Simaan immediately contacted his son-in-law, Dr Samweel Labeeb, who at the time was in his private clinic. He rushed to the scene. A first glance showed that the fall had fractured the man's skull, his thigh bone (femur) and the bones of his lower arm (radius and ulna). This was Dr Samweel's provisional diagnosis, but there was no opportunity to do an X-ray: 'When I arrived, I found Father Simaan praying, just touching Magdy and asking him what was wrong with him. I heard very loud cries [*sic*] of cracking, as if his bones were connecting again, connecting and connecting, and then he began to look up, and began to move, as if nothing had happened at all . . .'

And his reaction to this phenomenon? 'We have nothing like that in medicine. It's the power of the Lord.'[3]

Teaching and Training

Father Simaan did not promote trusting in 'the power of the Lord' among the *zeballeen* without also developing the mind. He doesn't subscribe to the idea that if God's Spirit works, there is no need to think: 'We eliminate ignorance: the whole aim is to overcome ignorance and the people learn – learn to read and write, learn to live, learn to read the Holy Bible.' Father Simaan and his pastoral team believe in fighting ignorance with all the resources at their disposal, but at first these were all too few. They had taken the first step of faith in the direction of educating the local children in 1975. Then Farahat's wife Su'aad had opened a tiny school of one class, containing two girls and three boys. It began to grow gradually, but lacked funding.

In 1986 a stranger was driving down the main road that goes past the Muqattam district. Although he was used to the unpredictable nature of Cairo traffic, he hit a rubbish cart. The impact threw a girl travelling in the cart on to the side of the road. The driver immediately got out of his car, attended to the girl – who wasn't badly hurt – and asked her where she lived. She directed him and he took her home. When he saw what conditions were like in the *zeballeen* area, it was a real eye-opener for him.

This newcomer turned out to be executive director of the Patmos Foundation, based in Helsinki, Finland. He tried to find out for the girl's sake what her community needed most, and the project he hit upon was a school. The Patmos Foundation then decided to build it and provide all the equipment, textbooks and exercise books.

They planned the building to form part of an enclosure around the church below the mountain. By the time it opened in 1993, 400 boys and girls were enrolled in general education classes. The building had five storeys to begin with, but the school eventually added a sixth level, and the number of pupils grew to around 500.

A reception department for pastoral care and instruction of children aged three to six helped them get used to being at school. Some families were without identity cards or official papers, so their children did not legally exist. This partly explains why they were not at government schools, but the higher profile of the newly built church school drew the government's attention to their plight. Within two or three years of its opening, the *zeballeen* found they could also get their children into government schools.

The role of the church school was to 'raise the children up out of the rubbish heap' – both spiritually and materially. Once they learnt to read and write they would then get help in reading the Bible. This was the priority. The secondary aim was to help them improve their standard of living.

The school includes a department for pastoral care and instruction of the deaf and dumb. There is also a department for the elimination of illiteracy, which can take children too old for regular school. This equips both boys and girls to read the Bible and join vocational training classes. Vocational training includes classes for domestic science, sewing, knitting and commercial fabric work for girls, and for carpentry, ironwork, electrician's work and leatherwork for boys.

For the older children vocational training is combined with spiritual training. The aim is that while they learn a craft, they also bond with the church, on the principle that 'those who bond with the church come to know God'. The aim is to strengthen each child's relationship with the Lord. Every week the younger children get a full 'spiritual day' that includes storytelling, Christian films and singing.

Disaster at Dawn

The opening of the school in 1993 was a great step forward for the community, yet the year ended with a stark reminder that other facilities were still lacking. At dawn on Tuesday, 14 December 1993, a landslide catapulted a section of the Muqattam Mountain down on to *zeballeen* homes.

Father Simaan and his workers immediately contacted the Patriarch, and he came to share the people's anguish. One twelve-year-old boy, Azaz, had been spending the night with his grandparents. When he arrived home, he found his mother and father, and all five brothers and sisters, crushed to death. The grief and chaos moved the Patriarch to tears. Yet he kept his wits about him and was quick to organize practical help. At least Azaz had his grandparents to turn to – they took him under their wing. Many families were now facing the winter with no home. So the Patriarch sent in food, clothing and blankets and set up financial help for survivors to build their homes again.

Despite all the rescue efforts, the final death toll was at least forty people. Medical help did not reach the injured quickly enough, because there was nothing available locally for the poor – only some private clinics for the rich. None of these would take in-patients, and the nearest hospital was Al-Hoseyn, 5 kilometres away. It stood near Al-Azhar University, a training centre for Muslim missionaries. The people who ran the hospital were Muslim fundamentalists, who are forbidden by their religion to touch pigs. Since the *zeballeen* kept pigs they called them 'pig-people', and they were nearly as reluctant to look after the 'pig-people' as they were to touch pigs.

The St Simaan Patmos Hospital

In fact the building of a hospital for Manshiyat Nasir was already under way, again with help from the Patmos Foundation. In 1993 a Finnish lady who was a field director for Patmos came and spoke with Dr Samweel, Father Simaan's son-in-law. She wanted to know if he would like to start a hospital. Next the executive director came. He handed Dr Samweel a blank sheet of paper and a pen, and asked, 'What are the things you would like to have in the hospital?' So Dr Samweel wrote down what he needed, contacted Finland, and the next day they told him they had agreed to all the equipment he asked for. Everyone was delighted.

They planned the hospital, like the school, to form part of an enclosure around the church below the mountain, down in the populated area. While the work on the hospital got under way, up on the mountain the conference hall that had been taking shape since 1991–2 was nearing completion. Beneath it was the Church of St Mark, which opened for worship in 1994.

On 12 April 1994 the Finnish ambassador, also Finnish Minister of Development and International Cooperation, came with the Patriarch to open the St Simaan Patmos Hospital. The *zeballeen* had done all they could to clean up the streets. They had covered them with sand and put up decorations everywhere. As the motorcade came by, doves were released in front of it; and when it came to a halt, the crowds around the Patriarch's car were so pressing that he couldn't get out of it for a quarter of an hour!

The Patriarch, the ambassador and other VIPs were shown around the new hospital building attached to the church below the mountain. They saw the out-patient clinics equipped with a laboratory for medical analysis, a diagnostic X-ray unit, and a theatre for major operations. As is usually the practice in a charitable institution in Egypt, there were both first- and second-class wards for in-patients. The patients in the first-class wards would pay more to help subsidize those who could not afford the full cost of treatment. The care of all patients was to be supervised by a team of specialist doctors.

The Mountain Amphitheatre

They then went up to 'the cavern' on the Muqattam Mountain. Again, the crowds were so pressing that entry through the main gates was impossible. Instead, the Patriarch and his entourage were let in through the connecting entrance of the Church of St Mark.

They emerged into a vast auditorium. It took the same name as the humble church that had been built there in 1986. Since then they had been gradually widening the mountain site of the original 'cavern' church – it had been a very simple structure when it opened in 1986. Now it covered an area of 10,000 square metres. They had gouged a great limestone amphitheatre out of the cliff face. Its deep beige walls were shot through at irregular intervals with lighter, sandy-coloured strata. The roof soared up 20 metres or more before opening out on to the sky.

The Patriarch and his entourage found themselves standing on a semi-circular platform in the heart of the great cavern, which acted as a focus for preaching and leading worship. The seating in front of them was fixed on semi-circular steps that radiated upwards away from the stage, making it look like a Roman theatre or a stadium. Since many meetings would be held in the evening, each step was sheathed in polished wooden bleachers fitted with foot-level lighting. The congregation rose in terraced ranks up to the cave mouth, where they sat etched against the stars.

To the congregation on the highest level, the visitors on the stage appeared as tiny figures. But they were not looking down but up, towards a gantry built out from the rock overhanging the stage into the centre of the auditorium. Suspended from it was a giant screen from which upwards of 12,000 spectators could follow the picture and voice of the Patriarch. What a transition from the early days of the church!

One visitor described the effect of this projection on the worship:

> I noticed above the stage a giant TV screen on which was projected the faces of the celebrants so that their words

could be better heard. When the liturgy was finished, a band and a singing group came on stage and we started into songs in modern Arabic. Then, would you believe, we were getting computer projection of the songs on the TV Screen [*sic*]. I could see the operator using his mouse and finding the words of each next song before it came full size on the screen. The people sang from their hearts.

Everyone was there: old, young, men, women, rich, poor. It was their place! It was modern! It was ancient! It was splendid! It was right on top of one of the poorest parts of Cairo.[4]

In his speech, the Patriarch commented: 'The presence of a very great number of people in this place is a very beautiful thing, but what is more lovely is that God should be in you and yourselves committed to God.'[5]

Father Simaan himself went through a reconsecration to God's service that same year. The Patriarch ministered to him what the Coptic Orthodox Church calls the 'grace of the *qomseya*'. This means the empowerment to be responsible for a group of priests. The title of 'Qomos' comes from the Greek word *hegumenos* or 'leader'.[6] The Patriarch gave Father Simaan this title in recognition of the fact that he was no longer a lone priest. He was now the most senior member of a team ministry. In June 1990 the Patriarch had ordained three other priests to serve in the area, two of whom had been assigned to the Church of St Simaan the Tanner: Father Boula Shawqy and Father Abraam Fahmy.

The Patriarch completed the ordained ministry team in June 1995 by adding a fifth priest, Father Rushdy. All this reflected the growth of the ministry on the mountain, which was by now one of the most active mission centres in the Middle East.

The church that met in the great auditorium was set to

become the largest worshipping congregation in Egypt and perhaps in the whole of the Middle East. It is the main focus for the fascination of the Muqattam Mountain, intimately connected with the charisma of Father Simaan. Like his hero of the tenth century, St Simaan, Father Simaan is short in physical stature yet carries a good deal of spiritual authority. Father Simaan was to be the main speaker at most of the spiritual meetings held in this hall. Each week he spoke to the people in a mixture of homely colloquial language and the classical Arabic in which the Bible is printed. Many of his talks found their way on to cassette tapes, which his hearers would buy and play often.[7]

7 SERVICE

The Retreat Centre

After the opening of the hospital and the auditorium Father Simaan and his co-workers put up a building on the narrow plateau facing the cavern. Here he could meet regularly with his ministry team to pray and plan. Despite the growth in their work, they were also willing to hire out the new building to other ministries and churches. They called it the St Simaan the Tanner Retreat Centre. On the top floor a fourth church was consecrated, named after the Angel and St John.

The team who met at the retreat centre included lay-workers who had graduated from the discipleship groups. Despite the difficulties of regular commitment to these, by sheer persistence, prayer and practical organization, many lay-workers began to emerge from them. They were not all equally qualified, but Father Simaan could find a use for most of them.

Those who joined discipleship groups had to be willing to attend the meetings, and be ready to serve Christ. There were three different phases. To succeed in the first level a person needed to give evidence that his spiritual life was firmly based. If he wasn't able to go on to the second level, he could still start to serve by taking a ministry appropriate to the first level. Some got to the second level, others to the third. Those lay-workers who completed the final level became *mukariseen* (consecrated workers).

The Service Cycle

A few of the 'consecrated workers' who had been in the discipleship groups from the very beginning could call on up to fifteen years of part-time training. They could join forces in their ministry with Onsi Labib, a committed lay-man who worked out a strategy for outreach. Their aim is nothing less than the 'revival and flourishing' of the Coptic Orthodox Church in Egypt.

With this aim, Onsi Labib has built up a network to reach other Coptic churches beyond the confines of the Muqattam Mountain region. The 'consecrated workers' all worship in their own local church and join in its ministry. Onsi is careful to build up good co-operative relations with the 'responsible authorities' in those churches. The methods the *mukariseen* use to expand their ministry are self-renewing. Onsi describes them in terms of a 'Service Cycle'.

First, there is 'soul winning for Christ' (2 Corinthians 5.19, 20); this involves 'personal work for winning the souls for Christ, whether inside or outside our congregations'. Second, there is 'steadfasting in Christ' (Acts 14.20-2). This involves following up those who have put their trust in Christ and to encourage and strengthen them. The aim is that they grow in their relationship with Christ, through weekly Bible Study groups that meet in churches or homes. Third, the *mukariseen* share in training members of these groups to practise different kinds of service. These include personal work, home visits, preaching and guiding Bible

Study groups. This stage Onsi calls 'growth in Christ', and he models it on 2 Peter 3.18 and Colossians 1.28–9. Fourthly (and this is the key to the continuation of the cycle) they must be 'preparing' lay-workers (Matthew 9.37–8).

The fruits of sending out these workers into the harvest field will include more soul winning, and a repetition of the cycle. Out of these lay-workers, leaders will arise – and this is the fifth and final stage, 'preparing leaders'. This follows the principle Paul gives to his 'dear son' in Christ, Timothy: 'the things you have heard me say in the presence of many witnesses entrust to reliable men who will also be qualified to teach others' (2 Timothy 2.2 *NIV*).

A similar cycle occurs not only in discipleship groups but also in caring for Christian families. The 'consecrated workers' aim to help families to 'lead a really effective Christian life and prepare them to serve other families in turn'. By strengthening relationships both within and between families the church community is built up. The process starts by laying a secure foundation at the beginning. Only well-trained members of the discipleship groups are entrusted with the delicate and sensitive task of nurturing the children in the Sunday schools. (Despite their name, these are usually held in Cairo on Fridays when the children have the day off from the government schools.)

Conferences are held for the members of all groups and all activities in the Service Cycle. When their outreach reaches a certain critical point, evangelistic conferences are held to which all active group members (no matter what level they are at) can invite their friends. The souls won to Christ in this way can in their turn go on to be made steadfast, to grow and be trained. However many stages they complete, the seeds are sown for another harvest.

New Halls and Churches

With the foundations for growth laid in this way, more and more people visited Muqattam for conferences, training sessions or for service. So there was wider scope to open more centres of worship and instruction. By 1997 a fifth church was added to the retreat centre. It was named after Anba Abraam (whose original name was Ibn Zara), who was the patriarch in whose time the mountain moved.

The five churches on the retreat site now include three halls. The retreat house can take about two hundred people and there is a special centre for the lay-workers there. There are also all the ingredients of a children's zoo or pets corner, with monkeys and doves and peacocks and parrots! A garden of remembrance was laid out in memory of Christ's passion at Gethsemane. A pony-tailed Polish sculptor called Mario goes all over the site using power tools to carve reliefs out of the rock. These help people to meditate on different scenes of Christ's life.

With the spiritual uplift that the retreat centre inspires, there are also vocational training units for young people, offering carpentry, ironmongery, wall or floor tiling and courses for budding electricians. For Father Simaan the basis of the work – whether 'spiritual' or 'vocational' – is the Holy Spirit. In his view it is the Holy Spirit who brings into being the very prayer meetings that uphold the work in all its forms. Of these there are at least four in a week, on Mondays and Wednesdays, on Thursdays after the open meeting, and on Fridays. This is where souls are prayed into the Kingdom. Without prayer none of them would come in.

The numbers attending today bear no comparison to what they were at the beginning. In the beginning, not one-quarter or one-fifth of these numbers came. Every month, every week, there is growth, because the Lord is working. This retreat centre is now visited by not less than 10–12,000 people every week. A very great number attend the meeting every Thursday, in the open-air amphitheatre cut out of the rock.

The Thursday meeting began originally in the church below the mountain, and then, when the church filled up, in the courtyard. After the courtyard they used the halls in the church. After the church halls filled up, they moved into the first conference hall, 2,000 metres square. After two or three weeks, even that began to fill up! After two or three months they needed a larger place, until they got the large auditorium (10,000 square metres) that by 1997 was three-quarters full. That will fill up too.

The retreat centre is itself seen as a miracle. As one Christian journalist commented in the magazine *Places in Egypt*, 'If you wanted to see the miracle of moving the mountain, come and see this miracle going on here and now.'

Father Simaan's vision for the future is that many souls will come back to Christ – since the Lord said 'I have many people in this city' (Acts 18.10). There are three or four communion services every week. Copts are given circular loaves for communion; these are broken up – hence they can't avoid leaving crumbs. When Father Simaan saw just how many crumbs the worshippers were leaving behind them, he confessed that God was fulfilling his promises to the letter in terms of the numbers attending.

He predicts that the day will come when every hall and church will have a video or a big screen working. Then the number of people who can benefit will multiply ten times over. God has provided a place that is unique not only in Egypt, but in any part of the world. In it are halls and churches, and with a television network they could reach everyone and everyone will hear – and God will work.

High Days and Holidays

People come to use the churches on site during fast days especially, and the big auditorium they worship in every Sunday. Many congregations from outside the area arrange outings and come and use the retreat centre churches for holding meetings and holy communion. In a typical holiday period there are four conferences every day with communion services in the churches. So the people take the opportunity of a retreat to sit with Christ on the mountain: 'I look to the hills! Where will I find help? It will come from the LORD, who created the heavens and the earth' (Psalms 121.1–2). The Lord Jesus himself used to take his disciples up a mountain, and people follow this example by taking time apart on the Muqattam Mountain for a spiritually refreshing retreat.

In the last two weeks of the half-term holidays in 1997, and the festival that rounds off the Muslim month of fasting, Ramadan, almost 120,000 people visited the retreat centre. There were many signs of God's Spirit at work – some people were moved to tears. What they sensed most strongly when they came to the mountain was that the Spirit of God was present, and working in them. People frequently came up to Father Simaan and asked, 'How can we make a start with Jesus?' or 'How can we know Christ?'

Nurture and Outreach

Although larger numbers come at holiday-time, people are always turning up even on working days. During the week they can attend meetings, conferences and services. On

Sundays there is a morning communion service attended by 1,000 people – sometimes many more. Some 4,000 come on Wednesdays to see a spiritual film. On Thursdays a special communion service is held with prayers for the open meeting in the evening. An average of around 7,000 people attended the open meeting in 1997.

Each week there are also group training sessions for lay-workers. All the groups link up with a priest. Father Abraam, for example, has five or six groups. Fathers Boula and Butros follow the same system, each having groups specially assigned to them for ministry training. This, at any rate, is the theory: in practice there are many demands on the priests' time, with many visitors coming to their offices to ask for their services. So they have to struggle to keep enough time for training.

There is also plenty of opportunity for outreach to the poor in the districts around Muqattam. In 1992 people all over Cairo had lost their homes in an earthquake that many delapidated buildings in the poorer districts could not withstand. Some buildings that seemed to survive the first shock later fell down in after-tremors that went on for days afterwards. International aid came into Egypt to help the destitute, and the government chose Muqattam as an area for resettlement. As their housing went up and the newcomers moved in, teams from the retreat centre visited them. They helped meet both material and spiritual needs. Many of the new arrivals, who had no personal commitment to Christ of any kind, began to come to the open meeting on Thursday evenings. Then they also went to the communion service on Sunday. People who had previously lost touch with God now became committed Christians. Some went deep in their study of the Bible and built up their own effective ministries.

Health and Refreshment

The distinctive needs of the district began to shape the approach of the Patmos Hospital ministry. Taking the Good Samaritan as a role model, Dr Samweel's team sought to meet the needs of the *zeballeen* as they found them. They soon discovered that there were distinctive needs that needed special attention. The first was traumatology: people transporting rubbish are often involved in accidents and collisions. The second group of problems could be called summer diseases, which cause diarrhoea and dangerous levels of dehydration in children.

A third problem that proved to be typical of the area was tuberculosis. This disease spread all over the district. Between 1994 and 1997 it was known to have spread worldwide, but in Muqattam the pre-conditions for it were not only rife, but also exacerbated by air pollution.

This problem stems from what Dr Samweel calls 'the real rubbish'. After you have taken out the plastic, the cardboard and the food, and everything else that is useful, the final, irreducible rubbish that cannot be recycled is still there. The *zeballeen* used to burn it and that caused the air pollution. If they don't burn it, there are huge quantities of 'real rubbish' lying around. If you put it in a big hole in the desert, for example, natural gas would come out of it – causing spontaneous explosions. The *zeballeen* try as much as possible to remove what they cannot recycle. This is often industrial waste. There are vehicles that take it away, but a small minority still prefer to burn it and this is very detrimental to the people.

Not only is the air pollution very bad, but also the living standard of the people is dropping again. Even if there were no air pollution, poverty and malnourishment would still create the pre-conditions for tuberculosis. Even people living in good accommodation grow weak if they can't afford to feed themselves properly.

Currently the living standard of the people is dropping because all their money is going on vehicles. Back in 1990 the Cairo governorate proposed a programme to mechanize the collection and transport of household waste. Lorries and pick-up trucks began to replace carts pulled by animals. For poorer people just making ends meet, this extra expense can tip the balance. They become significantly more susceptible to the illnesses which Dr Samweel finds in the area. This is not universal, but it is a recurring pattern.

For the first few years of its work the Patmos Hospital was just providing treatment, but from about 1996 they have been giving food as well. Day after day malnourished people are given milk, eggs, chicken and other meat. This has brought much better results, since usually it's not just the patient who needs treatment but the whole family. They all suffer from malnourishment and illnesses linked to it.

The hospital's change of emphasis towards dealing with chronic and long-term conditions has also involved it in work with the handicapped and with old people. The opening of an old people's centre in turn led to the inauguration of a programme of summer camps. This was widened to include all age groups. Every fortnight over a period of four months at least 500 campers go on summer conferences – a total of 8,000 people per year.

At first they used a place belonging to the Coptic Daughters of Mary, which is at Abu Sultan, near Fayid. This is in the Bitter Lakes region in the southern sector of the Suez Canal. But with increasing numbers coming on summer camps the church began to pray and plan for its own plot of land, near the Mediterranean coast west of Alexandria.

The site is 150 metres from the sea, at a place called Abu Talaat (near Al-Agamy).

The planned site can take about three hundred people. To give some idea of the scale of the need, we need only to take one example. A team of volunteers from more salubrious suburbs of Cairo organizes an annual school camp that runs for about twelve days. About four hundred children aged between four and fourteen take part. This is on top of their monthly outing, which might be to the pyramids or the zoo. It is a spiritual ministry, not just a trip. The volunteer team teach the children songs and stories about Jesus and show Christian films.

To understand the effect of this work we have only to think of Azaz, the twelve-year-old who lost his family in the landslide. He is growing up fairly normally, but there are times when very deep sadness within comes out in various forms of anti-social behaviour. When this happens, one of his uncles or the leader of his youth group takes him under his wing. He gets extra attention and, when necessary, discipline. In this way, the close-knit *zeballeen* community acts as a wider family for him. But sometimes he just needs to get away. For three summers in a row, from 1994 to 1996, he has gone with the school children on the summer camp. Each year, his friends on the team have found him more at peace with himself. They are praying that he will soon know Jesus, who can heal his inner wounds 'in a way that the world's greatest psychologist could never do'.[1]

Stewardship and Service

It's hard to imagine what it means to people who put up with the appalling stench of rubbish day in and day out, to be able to go to the sea. In fact, the church members felt so strongly about it that they committed themselves to buying the land, although they had to give sacrificially to do so. By the end of 1997 they had built about forty-two units on it, each taking four to seven people. This work costs around 300,000 Egyptian pounds, or £54,500 sterling. It is known as the Abu Sultan project. The church pays the money off in instalments and trusts the Lord to provide.

In general in its stewardship the church has had to learn how to handle large amounts of money in a responsible way. At one point an attempt was made by a relative of a member of the ministry team to siphon off money given to the church into his own private business. To learn to deal with this kind of problem is a painful but necessary part of the process of growing as a church – especially in an environment where so many people are very needy.

The Abu Sultan project is a good example of the benefits that a sacrificial investment can bring. The complete change of environment that the seaside centre offers helps the *zeballeen* and their families to become open to a programme with a spiritual aim. Many people who are far from God and don't know him, change when they go to the sea for four days. They leave behind the things that they resort to for consolation at the rubbish tip – such as beer and spirits – and start a relationship with the Lord.

What then? If someone comes to Father Simaan and asks to serve the Lord, he first checks to see if they have really made a beginning in the Christian life. He comes across many people who want to serve, without first beginning with Christ. Father Simaan feels that if they are missing this then they cannot give of themselves. Without Christ, they can't speak about Christ. They must begin with him and live with him.

Those who want to serve others and are sure of belonging

to Christ need to soak themselves in the Scriptures. After starting to put their teaching into practice the new believer can pray through the issues that come up, with a spiritual counsellor. In this way, Father Simaan and his team seek to guide the believer into the kind of service that is right for him or her.

He sees a great variety of opportunities for service. Intercessory prayer, personal work, preaching or evangelism – any of these can open up when the Holy Spirit is in control. Each type of service needs a certain gift. Some kinds of service require higher gifts – the Holy Spirit reveals what these are in response to the servant's commitment. Jesus promises that 'the Holy Spirit . . . will teach you everything and will remind you of what I said while I was with you' (John 14.26; cf. Luke 12.12).

The crucial thing for Father Simaan is that, as you read the Word of the Lord and pray, the Holy Spirit comes and fills you. After that, the Holy Spirit will use you greatly. 'Don't depend on your own power or strength, but on my Spirit' (Zechariah 4.6). 'Ministry in the flesh is of no benefit,' avers Father Simaan, 'but the most important element in ministry which makes it succeed, is the Holy Spirit which is in you and me.'

8 HEALING

Amputation or Prayer?

Word quickly began to spread of the healing miracles that were taking place among the workers in the Muqattam churches, and people began to bring their relatives and friends from outside the area to receive prayer for healing.

Caroline, a girl from Heliopolis or 'New Cairo', was suffering from a tumour in her upper tibia – the part of the shin bone just below the knee. Doctors who examined her in June 1991[1] found that this tumour was a malignancy called Ewing's Sarcoma. Caroline was only six years old, yet she was suffering from a rare and fatal condition. The only treatment for it at the stage it had reached was amputation.

This was the only recommendation she was given after going to France for specialist investigations; the doctors in Egypt agreed. While she was awaiting amputation, they gave her radiotherapy and chemotherapy. This resulted in her losing all her hair.

Yet Caroline's parents had faith that God could do something to save her leg. They went to the Coptic monastery of Abu Seifeyn, in Old Cairo – the same site that was rebuilt in the time of Patriarch Abraam. There they were advised to go and see Father Simaan in Muqattam. Hearing about the miracle of the mountain moving really helped to strengthen their faith that God can intervene in the present, as he did in the past.

They took Caroline to Muqattam, and through the ministry there she came to a personal relationship with God. And on 21 August 1994, Father Simaan prayed for her healing in the name of Christ. He then told the doctors to stop giving Caroline the radiotherapy and chemotherapy treatment, trusting that she had been healed.

Caroline's parents confirmed in faith that they did not want the amputation done. This was not a decision that can be taken lightly. Ewing's Sarcoma typically spreads from the leg to the liver and the brain, bringing death within about six months.

But Caroline is today a healthy girl, living at her family home in Heliopolis, or 'New Cairo'.

World Vision Award

By now, Father Simaan had been ministering at Muqattam for twenty years. Recognition for his ministry at Muqattam in all its forms came the year after Caroline's healing, in 1995. The Bible Society of Egypt recommended Father Simaan for a special presentation, citing his outstanding example in spiritual leadership. This recommendation led to the decision of World Vision International to give Father Simaan the Robert Pierce award. Its purpose is 'to provide recognition for those who have contributed in a significant way to the Kingdom of God'.[2]

Bruce McConchie, the Regional Director of World Vision in the Middle East, came and saw the church's ministry for himself. He describes the atmosphere in the Muqattam Mountain site on the night of the presentation:

The strains of 'He is Lord' rose from the cave as we strode in the Mokattam Coptic Orthodox church, on the outskirts of Cairo. As the auditorium came into view, the vastness was breathtaking. A huge arc of upward sloping terraces and seats to a charcoal grey crescent at the top where the cave opened to the sky and a single star. Ten thousand people could find seating in this place. The band, choir and congregation could now be seen and heard in one great crescendo of praise to the living Lord and Saviour.

We were deep inside the Mokattam Mountain as Father Simon Ibrahim gently guided me into the front rows of the auditorium. The worship continued. Time stood still as I reflected on what I had seen and heard during the previous few hours. It had been a non-stop affirmation of transformational development in all its variety and potential. The power of God was inescapable. The impact was evident in the thousands of people seated up to the sky behind me . . .

Father Simaan received the award in the presence of his congregation, his family and invited guests. It must have been a proud moment for his wife, Su'aad, who had supported him so faithfully in his ministry. She had held down a job as general secretary of a company while being active in church work and in bringing up their children, Albeer and Mary. Both of their children were now married and watching the presentation. Albeer had risen to become a company director, and Mary was helping to supervise the running of the Patmos Hospital with her husband, Dr Samweel.

Coptic priests representing the Bishop of Shubra El-Kheima diocese (who was abroad) came to attend the presentation of the award, as did the Director of the Egyptian Bible Society, Ramez Atallah, who for years had taken an interest in the ministry at Muqattam. The Reverend Jim Doust came to represent the Anglican Cathedral in Cairo.

Father Simaan was grateful for the recognition, but it also motivated him to pray, 'Create in me a clean heart, O God, and put a new and right spirit within me' (Psalms 51.10 *RSV*). He asked everyone present to pray that he would continue to be strengthened and encouraged by the Lord. '*Places* – like Muqattam,' he said, 'do not satisfy the hearts of men. Only God satisfies the hearts of men. Therefore you can say, "I live, yet not I, Christ lives in me!"'

Transformed Lives

The thousands who attended left the auditorium with that challenge ringing in their ears and – he hoped – resonating in their hearts. The gospel continued to make a big impact on people's lives. The goodness of God continued to be seen in the ministry of the church, the hospital, the kindergarten and the lower primary school. His abundant provision was seen in vocational training activities and encouragement for small businesses. Lives were being transformed by these projects.

One example was Jehan, a girl from a very poor family who had graduated from the church school. She joined the Vocational Training Workshop and became skilled in making attractive handicrafts from recycled cloth. Her work helped greatly to raise the standard of living in her family. Jehan became one of the first *zeballeen* girls to travel. She went abroad to represent the Workshop at international conferences concerned with recycling. The Workshop and other projects to kick-start small businesses were playing a vital role in a population in and around the mountain that had now reached 40,000 people.

The Impossible Dilemma

Miracles of healing continued to occur. For example, there was an urgent crisis to face in the case of a young couple – Nahid and her husband, Mahir.

Nahid found that she was losing weight rapidly. When it had dropped from eleven to seven and a half stone, she went to a doctor, who immediately took blood tests. Nahid was also suffering from terrible headaches. She was given antibiotics, but it wasn't long before the doctor referred her to Ayn Shams hospital.

After being given the usual X-rays a consultant told Mahir that Nahid needed a brain scan. The equipment for this was not available in the hospital so Mahir had to take Nahid to a specialist centre. They then went back to the consultant, who told Mahir that the situation was extremely serious. He said that Nahid had a swelling on the outer covering of the brain, known as an extradural haematoma. This external symptom was linked to an internal problem in the brain. There was a major artery in the brain that had an aneurism – a condition that causes sudden dilatation or ballooning of the wall of the blood vessel. Eventually it bursts, causing haemorrhaging in the brain. The rupture was likely to happen within seventy-two hours.

Doctors also told Nahid that they would have to perform open heart surgery. Tests had shown that she was suffering from cardiomyopathy – a condition affecting the muscles of the heart which can in some cases necessitate a heart transplant. Not long after they told her this she lost consciousness for a time and her husband, Mahir, found himself in an impossible dilemma.

The doctors told him that to have any chance at all of saving Nahid, they must do operations on both the heart and the brain. One operation without the other would not work. It was not enough just to operate on the valves in the heart that were malfunctioning. If they did not also deal with the dilated artery in the brain, then the brain would haemorrhage within seventy-two hours.

Yet to agree to this double operation was a huge responsibility. Mahir was told in no uncertain terms that the risks of such an operation going wrong were so great that the outcome was doubtful in the extreme. It was possible that even if the surgery succeeded, Nahid might be left paralysed in both legs. The area the surgeons could safely work on in the brain was no more than 2.5 square centimetres in area.

Mahir told the doctors that he and Nahid had a Christian faith: that if this was impossible for human beings, it could be possible for God. The doctors hadn't considered this point of view at all and were certainly not convinced by it. But they did agree to have Nahid moved from intensive care to a cardiac ward.

When Mahir called Father Simaan to come and see them, the first thing he said to Mahir was this: 'Do you pray or not?' Mahir said to him, 'I used to pray, but I don't these days.'

'Why don't you pray?'

'After I got married I just stopped praying,' he confessed.

'Do you have faith, or not?'

'I have faith that God will heal her.'

Father Simaan had come while Nahid was unconscious. The heart monitoring equipment was taken off her, and

Father Simaan put his hand on her face, making a cross upon it. He brought a cup of water, prayed over it, and put it to one side. Then he prayed for her.

Nahid appeared to be asleep. Father Simaan went and got the water and poured it on her face three times. 'After that,' said Mahir, 'our Lord was glorified and the miracle took place.' Nahid regained consciousness. Father Simaan then spoke to Nahid: 'As Christ said, "Pick up your bed and walk," I say to you, pick up your bed and walk!'

Father Simaan then told Nahid to go home. She had been used to having four injections every hour, and another injection every four hours. In the hospital she had had numerous injections of antibiotics, and there had been no response to them. But now Father Simaan was telling her to leave the hypodermics behind her and go home! In the most natural and unaffected way possible, she got up and – with Mahir's help – packed up her things and went home.

All this happened on Friday, 9 August 1996. Father Simaan had arrived at noon. They went home at one. The surgeon had informed Mahir that he needed a day to prepare for the operation. Since the hospital only did operations on Saturday, Sunday and Monday, that meant they had to decide by Friday or Saturday at the latest.

By 1.15 pm on Friday Mahir and Nahid made their decision: there would be no operation. They phoned the doctor from home and told her that Nahid had been healed by faith. The doctors were totally unconvinced and decided they must be very ignorant people. How could Nahid have just discharged herself when the X-rays showed that she had an aneurism in the brain on top of needing new valves in the heart? But that is just what Nahid had done.

Yet the threatened haemorrhage never took place, and

Nahid made a full recovery. She came to give her testimony at Muqattam on 9 September, with her husband Mahir and her small son. Since she had been unconscious much of the time, Mahir had to fill in many aspects of the trial they had gone through. She had not even known about the life-threatening aneurism in the brain, but she was now completely free of all its symptoms, such as the severe headaches she had suffered from.

Such testimonies showed those who heard them that trials do not have to lead to despair. 'Nothing is impossible with God' (Luke 1.37). The believers at Muqattam saw that, by turning every problem into prayer, God could make them 'more than conquerors' (Romans 8.37) over everything.

These testimonies also affected their view of death. In the Western world, people are frightened of talking about death. When someone famous (such as Princess Diana) dies suddenly, it sends shock-waves around the country, although in many ordinary families people often have small and private funerals. In the East, by contrast, people drop everything when someone they are acquainted with dies. Men leave their place of work and women dress up in black to go and sit with the bereaved family. Death in Egypt has a higher profile and people can display great, almost uncontrollable, emotion in public funerals.

But the believers at Muqattam began to sense that bodily death did not have to be seen through terrible tears, loss and anguish – but could be understood as the process of being transferred from one state of existence to another. A grey-haired priest present at Nahid's public testimony reminded the listeners of how Jesus said of the daughter of Jairus, the synagogue ruler, 'The child is not dead, but asleep' (Mark 5.39). Then he said to her, 'Little girl . . .

arise' (verse 41), just as if he were waking her up from sleep. Sleep here means bodily death. It is sin that is *really* death.

If we do not hear God's voice calling us in this life, we will hear it on the day of judgement. The miracle God really wants to do is the miracle of raising us from the death of sin.

If you are ill in Egypt, you can spend a huge sum to get the services of a well-known surgeon, for instance. But many people, like Nahid and Mahir, can testify that God was able to raise them up not just from the bed of sickness, but from death itself – freely, without charge or payment. Even this, to them, is only a sign of something infinitely greater. To trust in the blood of Christ is to be truly raised: raised not merely from the death of the body, but of the soul.

Out of the Pit

On 16 October 1996 a young doctor gave a testimony at a meeting in Muqattam. He explained how his preoccupation with healing the body for a time led him away from the Lord. But God intervened, and turned his priorities upside down:

'I was suffering from three slipped discs in the lower part of my back. A doctor told me to rest. After five weeks, he said, I should be able to go back to my normal everyday life.

'What was my everyday life like? I had known the Lord for about fifteen years, having had an experience of meeting him personally. Yet after starting work I found little time for him. I told myself, this is not like the time you were at school, or university. Now you are in the world of work, it's completely different. You can't expect to have time for ministry. Anyway, I told myself, medicine is a kind of ministry – and this is how I quieted my conscience.

'There came the time when I was afflicted with three slipped discs. For the whole five weeks that the doctor had told me to rest I felt unable to get up from my bed except to go to the toilet. At the end of that time I got into a chair. After precisely five minutes I felt a sharp pain in my back that transmitted itself down one leg. I told the doctor what had happened, mentioning that I was now beginning to feel pain on my right side when previously it had only been on my left. This doctor was a well-known specialist in bone disease. He told me, "Look, you can do one of two things. Either take to your bed and stay there for another two months, or – if you're the kind of man who earns a thousand dollars a day – I can do an operation for you tomorrow morning. It won't cure the problem instantly, but it could speed up the time it takes to recover."

'These words discouraged me very much. I couldn't get up from my bed, and got depressed. My brother was going out to see a priest, so I told him, "Tell the priest that I'm ill."

'When the priest came I had two questions for him. They were not about healing. Although I was a believer, it wasn't the issue of healing that was occupying my mind. What I wanted to know was, "Does God want to say something to me through this illness?" And secondly, "Where is the wisdom of God in leaving me unable to work and support my family?"

'[Father Simaan] came and I asked him,

'"Is there anything you want to say about my illness?"

'"No," he said. This reply seemed to me a let-down.

'"Is my illness something to do with my spiritual condition?" I asked.

'"I don't know." At this I really felt as if I were in the pits of depression. But he added,

'"You should ask God, and he will tell you." Then the priest asked a question of his own: "Do you believe that Jesus Christ heals you?"

'He prayed, quoting two Bible verses. Then he commanded:

'"Get up." And I got up.

'"Move your head." I moved it.

'"Walk to the other end of the flat." I went.

'"Come back." I came.

'At the end he said, "Congratulations, God has cured you!" I went and kissed him [a culturally normal thing for men to do in the Middle East, and particularly as a mark of respect to a priest]. I showed him to the door, and hesitated. A little uncertainly, I asked, "Can I move about now?"

'"You can run and jump!" he replied.

'Run and jump! I was exhilarated. I went and shaved off my beard, got dressed and found my wife. I wanted to go and greet my father and brother. I spent two hours bumping up and down in a car seat. I wasn't on a fixed seat: it was bumping up and down.

'I was taught in my medical training that if I put a lot of weight on one disc it would transmit pressure to the next – and if I put a great deal of pressure on the spinal cord (for example, by jolting up and down) in the condition that I had this could lead to a paralysis of the leg.

'So I felt that people seeing me like this were bound to try to stop me moving around. I knew that even when I found the courage to tell people that I was healed, people would tell me, "Even so, take it easy – don't do this or that." But I was determined not to give in to that pressure.

'This determination was tested when I felt some pain, and it came back, on and off. I took this as a challenge, and read right through the Gospel of Matthew, highlighting in yellow all the statements made about healing. Armed with these verses, I felt equipped to fight a spiritual battle. This struggle went on for four days as I insisted – no matter what the devil might tempt me to believe – that God had healed me. At the end of that time, the pain finally stopped. I have now been living a very, very normal life for the past four months, without any recurrence of the illness.

'Remarkable as it was, though, this healing was not merely God touching my body. Much more powerful than the physical healing was the fact that God gave me joy in my life. This joy meant more to me than anything else, and so I became open once again to ministry. I offered everything back to the Lord – the hospital, my work, my leisure time. I said to him, "Take my hand and lead me anywhere you want – anywhere at all. All that matters to me is that I should be in your kingdom."'

9 NEW HEARTS

Eventually, news of 'the power of the Lord' at work at the Muqattam Mountain spread not only in Egypt, but also abroad. Because of their Christian faith, Copts face barriers to promotion and career opportunities in their homeland. Therefore they have scattered all over the world in their search for better opportunities for work or greater freedom to put their faith into practice. Some Egyptians rise to great prominence abroad. From 1992 to 1997 the Secretary-General of the United Nations was Dr Butros Ghali, a Copt. Among the Muslim community, Mohamed Al Fayed, the owner of Harrods, and his late son, Dodi, are household names in Britain.

To the Copts, an equally famous name is Sir Magdy Yaqoub, who has carried out many successful heart transplants in England. His prowess as a surgeon was well known to the family we are going to meet. They appreciated too the skills of Dr John Mitchell, a consultant heart specialist. This is a story about a brother who followed their advice – and his sister who found a different route to healing.

Hany's Trauma

Like many emigrant Coptic families, they were spread out over at least three countries: a nucleus in Cairo, a brother working in Germany (whom we will call Hany), and a sister who had lived in London since she was thirty (we will call her Sara). In 1994, doctors in Germany discovered that Hany was suffering from heart disease. The diagnosis (as for Nahid in the last chapter) was cardiomyopathy. When he came to see his sister in London, she was horrified to find him in a deep state of depression concerning his illness. Soon he was in hospital, his life hanging by a thread. He was totally reliant on various pieces of cardiac equipment to stave off the threat of heart failure.

Sara was very aware how serious the situation was and realized that her brother probably didn't have long to live. At the same time, she couldn't come to terms with what was going on, or face up to the future. The next day she set off in her car to see Hany in the hospital, and on the way her car broke down. Sara felt deep despair. It seemed like the last straw. She found herself praying from the depths of her heart, 'Lord, I am worn out. I'm exhausted, stuck out here between home and hospital. Do something, anything.' She was in floods of tears, and yet for the first time had a strange feeling that God *would* do something.

Sara scarcely remembers how she got the car repaired. When she finally did get to the hospital she had no idea what condition she would find Hany in. She was horrified to see on the monitor screen that his heart had swollen up. The doctors explained to her that there was a dilatation ('ballooning') of the walls of the blood vessels. To Sara, it looked like an ocean of water. Hany desperately needed a new heart, but he was also suffering from an infection that gave him a high temperature. So it looked as though they couldn't go ahead with a transplant that day anyway. Sara stayed a while with Hany, then went home.

The hospital lost no time in giving Hany antibiotics to

try to control the infection. This process could have taken up to forty-eight hours. Yet at eight o'clock that evening Sara's phone rang. It was the hospital, asking her to come in. They were going ahead with Hany's operation.

So after going through the agonies of uncertainty over what would happen to Hany, Sara suddenly found events moving very fast indeed. She was glad that God could see she could stand the suspense no longer, and was going to act decisively. This was a tremendous relief to her, but the whole build-up to the operation had been so traumatic that she couldn't imagine ever coping with such an experience again.

The operation was difficult and delicate. But when the doctors checked and rechecked the condition of Hany's new heart, they pronounced the operation a success. In due course, they discharged him, and Sara returned to her normal busy life. About a year later, just when she had reached the point of thinking that the whole episode was safely behind her, her own health took an abrupt nose-dive.

It happened on 25 November 1995. 'I felt completely shattered, unable to move. I couldn't even lift a piece of paper. My body began to cause me pain day and night. When I tried to get up from my bed, I couldn't.' This went on 'day after day after day'. Finally she was admitted to hospital, but the doctors didn't come up with any clear results. After a thorough examination and X-rays, their comments were guarded. 'There's something wrong,' they admitted, 'but we don't know what it is.'

Sara went to a second hospital and then a third. In the end one doctor felt ready to commit himself to a diagnosis. 'I will see you tomorrow morning,' he promised (the next day was a Sunday), 'and God willing I will give you all the details.'

During this whole period of twelve days Sara had been

unable to sleep, or eat, or drink. She couldn't move at all
without assistance. At last, when the doctor came the following day, he did the same checks all over again. Then he
suggested a new test. 'We'll do a cardiogram.'

Sara protested, 'No, there's nothing wrong with my
heart. Up to ten days ago, I was active twenty-four hours a
day. I have the housework, I have children, I have private
work . . .'

'Nevertheless,' he insisted, 'we will do a cardiogram and
an X-ray.'

After the cardiogram, the doctor did not return to Sara.
Instead he phoned the cardiac unit where her brother had
been. He wanted to talk to a doctor urgently – and even
though it was Sunday, he insisted that he must admit Sara.
Sara's sister-in-law went with her in the ambulance. She is a
doctor, and they gave her a hypodermic needle. Sara recalls
the ambulance men saying, 'If anything happens, if she
can't stand the journey, then you can give her this injection.
If she can make it there without, all well and good.'

Sara went into the cardiac unit on 20 December. By this
time, her condition had deteriorated. The doctor who
examined her tried to ask her questions about it, but to her
frustration she found she couldn't reply. 'I couldn't complete
a single sentence. I couldn't tell him what had happened.
The doctor brought a piece of equipment which monitors
the heart. He looked and said, "Unfortunately the heart is
really not functioning well . . ."'

For four days Sara stayed in the observation room, wired
up to every conceivable gadget, 'monitoring blood, monitoring everything'.[1]

'Everything I did I had to do in bed, with all the equipment
around me, left and right. Of course what had happened to
my brother had given me experience of these things and I

knew I was following the same path. I saw the heart on the monitor screen, how it had swollen up, and there was nothing to be said.' Yet still there was no definite diagnosis. After four days' observation, Sara was discharged and told how many times a week she should return to the hospital.

For the first week Sara went along for routine checks and that was all, but in the second week the pronouncement was made. 'Unfortunately', she was told, 'you have the same condition as your brother.'

Despite everything that had happened, Sara could hardly believe the news. Somehow she had thought that things would be different for her. So when she heard the diagnosis she went into complete shock – she just couldn't accept that she had the same condition. Dimly, as if he were talking about someone else, she heard the doctor say, 'Unfortunately, the left side of the heart is no longer functioning and you are depending on the right.' When the truth began to dawn, she wondered where these words left her – in all the pressures and busyness of life with her body tiring her out every day?

All this time, Sara's weight was dropping. She had been about ten and a half stone when she went into hospital on 20 December, and within a couple of weeks she had lost about half a stone. She lay motionless in bed while the doctor tried to explain her condition to her, but she was so worn out, she couldn't take it in. She started to say to him, 'Suppose, in the worst possible outcome –' but couldn't make herself finish the sentence. The doctor said that all they could do was use medication to try to preserve the other side of the heart.

'All right,' Sarah managed to say, 'I'm not a doctor, I don't have experience, I don't have any idea of what is happening. If there was someone else in this room who was in

100 per cent good health, what would be the difference between him and me?'

The doctor looked at her and said, 'If we had a scale from one to ten, I would give you five.'

With that, he left. Sara stayed in bed, unable to move, until he came back three days later. She was given medicine that was supposed to help her get up and walk, but still she couldn't get up. Every day she would ask herself, 'When will I be able to move?' and her son would say to her, 'Not now, not yet'.

Sara feared asking questions, but in the end she did. When the doctor came to see her again, she demanded to know: 'If the medicine doesn't work, what will happen?'

Sara's Decision

She knew already what the answer would be, but she needed to hear him say it. He replied, 'You would need an operation.' Yet to hear her fear put into actual words made her even more afraid. She could see herself enduring the traumas of the same treatment as her brother, but perhaps without such a good outcome. Yet she felt within herself a certain reserve of faith. She had always gone to the Coptic church in London, and to many other churches, but now she couldn't go anywhere. So she made a direct, personal appeal to God. 'I found myself saying, "Lord, you allowed my brother to go through these things, but I don't need an operation. I need a miracle."' At this point Sara was sent home to await the operation.

The doctor told her, 'The most you should do is go as far as the kitchen, make a sandwich, and go back and rest. You should not do more than that. You shouldn't be on your own; there must be somebody staying with you.'

'You mean I shouldn't get up, even to take medicine?'

'No.'

Sara said nothing more and followed these instructions. In January she went into hospital and saw Dr Mitchell. She began to go to the hospital every week, and every month they did the same X-ray. Yet there was no improvement at all. Finally Dr Mitchell, as her cardiologist, in consultation with the hospital surgeon Sir Magdy Yaqoub, advised Sara to have a heart transplant.

This was a road Sara simply could not face. She had gone down it once, vicariously, for her brother, and knew that the operation had succeeded. Yet she couldn't face all that stress and uncertainty again. What was the alternative?

She kept praying for an answer, but it did not come at once. Yet the day came when, as she prayed, it came to her that she should go to Egypt. 'I was always praying, but there came the moment when I felt that this is what I should do. Many times when I prayed nothing happened, but this time I said to myself, "I must go. There is something in Egypt I need." What that was I couldn't have told you.'

Sara began to feel this way in June. She had followed the medical regime in London for about eight months and took the medicine until the last possible moment. Yet she 'just knew' there was something in Egypt she needed. So she booked a flight, went to the hospital for the regular X-ray and told the doctor, 'I want to go to Egypt.'

'Why?' he asked.

'There's something I must see to there.'

'How long will it take?'

'Ten days.'

'Who is going with you?'

'My daughter.'

'You'll be away ten days, not one month?'

'No,' she reassured him.

On a Wing and a Prayer

So Sara went ahead and booked the flight. She didn't take any medicine with her, or any documents to show what she was suffering from. She was even afraid to tell anyone on the plane, since she wanted to keep her quest to herself. 'All the time on the plane, I was saying, "Lord, don't let anything happen. If anything happens at all, people might find out what I've got."'

Sara arrived in Cairo on 22 June 1996. Following doctor's orders, she had booked her return flight for 30 June. But when her family in Cairo saw her condition for themselves, they said, 'No, you can't possibly travel in this state – you must stay.' So Sara went to the airline office to try to delay her return flight, but there was nothing available. Every day she went to the airline office and every day they said, 'There are no return flights available, none at all – apart from the day you've already booked, everything is booked up.' That, it seemed, was all there was to it. She gave up trying to change the ticket and told herself, 'If I must go back on 30 June, then I must.'

But she knew that there was something special she needed that she was searching for. She turned to her family and said, 'Look, everyone, I need someone to pray for me. Yet I cannot explain to you what it is that I need. I feel the need to go to a monastery – but I can't go unless someone helps me.'

All Sara's friends and loved ones came and said, 'Ah, we could find so-and-so for you, this father or that father could pray.' But they didn't come. So what could she do?

One day they decided to go together to a monastery. Sara really wanted to go to the monastery of St Mina, but they took her to a monastery that was nearer. Then one of her relations spoke to one of the monks, saying, 'There is a lady with us who is ill. She has come from London, and we need someone to pray for her as she is worn out.' The reply was dismissive: 'But she has Magdy Yaqoub over there!'

These words really annoyed her. She was seething as she left the monastery, and felt badly let down. 'Did I come here for that?' she asked herself. 'If I had wanted Magdy Yaqoub, would I have come all the way to Egypt? I came for something else.' Sara was full of sadness and pain, and a sense of loss. She arrived home from the monastery in a state of collapse, unable to do anything.

She had a sleep, and after that went into the kitchen. Sara thought, 'That's it. I'm not going to any other monasteries.' She was going to confirm her flight for the 30th, and that was that. But by the time she came out of the kitchen the phone was ringing. It was the airline office to say that they had transferred her booking from 30 June to 22 August.

Sara was silent. She didn't say a thing, but she thought to herself, 'All right. I won't tell everyone what I was going to say about going back and not wanting to go to a monastery.'

The Miracle

Soon after that, a member of her family said to her, 'One of the fathers is available and he can pray for you.' Sara snapped back, 'OK, everyone, find me someone, anyone!' She tried to sleep that night, but she couldn't. How she prayed! She stayed in the presence of the Lord waiting, listening, asking.

'Someone listening in would have been sure that there was someone with me.'

Sara cried out from the depths of her heart. Her tears were flowing, not just from her eyes but from her heart. She reached the point when she said to God, 'All right, don't do this miracle for my sake. I am coming to you for this miracle, and I am clinging on to you. If I have sinned, and don't deserve it, do it for the sake of the person who prays for me – whoever that may be. Do your miracle with me. Don't let me go back on the 22nd without finding someone. I sense that this is something I must receive before I go. I can't come back here again.

'You say, if I only had faith like a mustard seed – but I haven't got even this, my faith is very weak. So please strengthen my faith so that I can ask this thing from you.'

Sara cried such tears 'no human being could imagine'. When she awoke, she was taken by surprise by a phone call telling her that a priest was going to come and pray with her the very next day. That was to be 30 June – the very day she was originally supposed to fly back to London.

The priest arrived. Sara didn't know him, but it was Father Simaan. He sat next to her and asked, 'What's the story?'

So she told him her troubles from beginning to end.

He said to her, 'Do you have faith?'

Sara replied, 'I came here, so that shows I have faith to ask for anything.'

He took her at her word. 'All right,' he said. 'If you have faith, what do you want from our Lord? Do you want a new heart? If that's what you want, ask for a new heart. Do you want a new heart?'

She nodded.

So he said to her quite simply, 'That's all there is to it

then – you will have a new heart.' He prayed for her, sprinkled water on her, and anointed her with oil.

Then Father Simaan said, 'It's finished. Get up and go out. Go down the stairs.'

'All right,' Sara replied, uncertain what to think.

At that, they fell silent. Sara said goodbye to Father Simaan and kissed his hand. On his way out, he said to her, 'There is a meeting you can come to.' She agreed to it, and they arranged that she should come on Saturday to Muqattam.

In Egypt, appointments are not regarded as binding unless they are reconfirmed. In fact, Sara had no real intention of going. As far as she was concerned, that was the end of it. 'He had prayed for me, and I didn't know what to do next. I went into the room and found a chair next to the bed. I went in and, without thinking about it, even though I had been forbidden by the doctors to do this and that, I picked up a chair that was next to the bed.'

'Auntie, don't do that!' It was one of Sara's nieces, telling her off for disobeying the doctors' orders.

'Be quiet!' Sara snapped back – before she could stop and think about what she was saying.

'I don't know why I said that to her. I went and picked up the chair and put it back in its place. I was rather amazed, but not believing. After that I sat on the sofa and my son came to me.'

Sara said to him, 'I have a request.'

'What is it?' he asked.

'I want to find someone to do me a cardiogram.' Sara felt torn between two things: she wanted to hold on to her faith – perhaps God had *really* done something for her – and at the same time, she wanted to see a doctor, in the hope that he would tell her something more concrete.

'Can't you go when we get back to London?' her son asked.

'No, I want to go to a doctor now.'

Sara wanted to hear information from a doctor, but at the same time there was an apprehension inside her about her lack of faith. She feared that it could ruin everything.

So she went to a doctor and waited to get a response. She said to the Lord, 'I am coming to strengthen my faith.'

She went in to see the doctor. The nephew who was with her said, 'This is my aunt, who is staying with us. Her brother has a heart condition and we would like you to check that she has not inherited a similar problem.'

The doctor asked a series of questions, to all of which the answer was, 'No.' They included this one:

'Do you feel anything when you exert yourself?'

Sara replied, 'No.'

'All right, I'll do an examination.'

The X-rays showed that the heart was in perfect working order. Sara didn't know what to say. She tried to put words into his mouth – anything that would contradict that. But she couldn't. The doctor averred that each part of the heart was working perfectly.

'What is the size of the left ventricle?' Sara asked.

'You can see it on the screen.'

'I know, I'm sorry I'm asking all these questions, but from my experience with my brother I need to make sure.'

'Go ahead, ask away.'

'What about the heartbeat? Is it as it should be?'

The heart rate, it turned out, was sixty-six, as compared to a normal rate of between seventy and ninety. To the doctor, it was as near normal as possible: in fact he regarded anything above sixty as a bonus. And despite all Sara's attempts to drag out of him any kind of negative diagnosis, the doctor insisted that no more tests were needed. 'There is nothing wrong with your heart whatsoever,' was his final verdict.

Sara got up and went out. The first thing her son said to her when she got home was, 'That was wrong. You should have told the doctor what you had so that he could test it properly.'

'Be quiet! Not a word!' said Sara peremptorily.

In the end, she asked a male relative to ring the doctor and let him describe what had happened and confirm it. It was Dr Magid Ramses, who practises in Roxy, Heliopolis. (Heliopolis is a suburb of Cairo.) So the relative phoned him and asked if the X-rays he had done showed that the heart was functioning perfectly.

'One hundred per cent,' Dr Ramses confirmed.

So the relative said, 'All right, I want to tell you something.' And he then explained the background to the case, and that Sara had been having treatment for the past nine months.

The doctor was very surprised. He said, 'I don't know which of you to believe. All I can say to you is that the heart I saw on the screen is 100 per cent healthy. You can come and take a report if you like, and take it to any other doctor.'

At last Sara fully believed that the miracle had really happened. She was healed! So now it was time to act . . .

That same day she started cooking; and it was the first day since November in which she didn't need bedrest.

She began to tell her family, but there was such a storm of emotions inside her that she was afraid that if she tried to tell them what had happened, she might not be able to get it across. How could any human being explain that kind of thing? It was so strange that the miracle had happened the very day she was supposed to go back to London, on 30 June.

She started to say to God, 'Lord, I should have been in

London by now. What a great thing you did for me, in putting off my journey so that the miracle could take place in me.' Yet she could still hardly believe it, and all the time she was praying she wanted to go back to her doctor and say, 'Examine me, and tell me your opinion.'

The miracle happened on Tuesday, and she was supposed to go to the retreat centre on Muqattam on Saturday. She arranged to leave that day by car at eight o'clock in the morning, so as to make an early start and avoid the worst of the Cairo traffic.

A Narrow Escape

When the day came she went into the kitchen with one of her relatives who was going to drive her to Muqattam. As she was making a cup of coffee she noticed that there was a smell of gas.

She told her relative and he said, 'Well, we'd better test the gas bottle.' He checked the bottle and the oven and found nothing. As Sara was trying to close the window there was an ear-splitting explosion from the oven. All the glass in the kitchen shattered. The sink fell on top of the gas bottle. The gas bottle fell on the ground and started to leak. Sara screamed and shouted, 'Get out, get out!' as she knew what would happen – another explosion.

Then God was glorified. As Sara heard the sound of the gas escaping, she saw that a bottle she used for storing water in had fallen too. The water poured out and stopped the fire reaching the gas bottle.

'The two of us were shattered. We staggered out of the kitchen, I slumped into a chair, and so did my relative. I said to him, "That's it, I'm not going to the monastery. I can't face getting into a car and you can't possibly drive."

115

'We stayed like that for half an hour. After that, he said to me, "No, we must go through with it."

'I told him, "I can't, I've had it." I was so shocked I said, "What is it about going to the monastery that something like that should happen? The first monastery I went to they brushed me off, telling me to go to Magdy Yaqoub. If the miracle hadn't happened I would have been really angry about this. This is very strange – it doesn't make sense."'

But they went through with it. They went up to the retreat centre at Muqattam and prayed there that same Saturday, the day they had agreed upon. Sara told Father Simaan the story about the gas bottle and how, even despite this, she had come to the monastery and completed her errand. She was astonished to see him laughing and shaking his head, and saying, 'This is something strange, this is unique! God has *definitely* given you a new heart!'

Sara's Testimony

Sara was asked to give her testimony at the meeting:

'And as you see I am standing before you now, and I thank our Lord for giving me this new opportunity and that circumstances have permitted me to come. If there is one thing I have learnt from this trial, that is that if you ask something from God, you must ask for it in faith. We may well ask for miracles, but unfortunately as human beings we don't have within ourselves the power of faith. Yet even the episode with the gas bottle encouraged me to keep holding on to the Lord to the end, because I did not want to return empty. And in fact God did work in me to do his miracle . . . so that I could go back and testify to it wherever I go.'[2]

10 *THE VISION*

Father Simaan is now the grey-bearded, plain-spoken leader of a powerful team ministry of preaching, healing and exorcism. It is hard to get an interview with him (and even to get material for a book such as this), not because he is standoffish – far from it – but because, as he puts it, 'God is doing so much'. There is hardly time for him to finish describing something God has already done before we are interrupted by a fresh need about which God wants to do something.

A mobile phone rings as I am asking about Sara (the woman described in the previous chapter) who came from London with heart disease. Father Simaan disappears into his outer office, where there is a non-Christian in need of exorcism. She has an evil spirit which has cut her off from relations with her husband and periodically throws her to the ground in a dead faint, which can last for several hours. She is standing with one leg sticking out in an involuntary pose.

Father Simaan rebukes the spirit in a loud voice, stamps his feet, strikes her with two fingers of his hand and calls for water. This he flicks sharply into her face and prays for her in the name of Christ and in the name of the cross. She is immediately released from the evil spirit in front of her friends. She asks how she can stop the spirit coming back, and Father Simaan tells her to pray always in the name of Christ and in the name of the cross. Within a few minutes, the encounter is over and the lady leaves.

All this is done in the most natural, matter-of-fact way as if it were an everyday occurrence. Father Simaan returns to his desk and we go back to the question about Sara's healing.

Father Simaan refers me to Dr Samweel, who tells me that Sara's condition was 'familial' – just like her brother, she had inherited it. Since she chose not to have a transplant, the disease would probably have been terminal. Yet her heart was changed (in more ways than one) following Father Simaan's prayer.

Continuity and Change

There is nothing contrived about the contemporary Father Simaan, any more than there was when he was simply known as Brother Farahat. He still has the same 'silent' prayer-partner who supported him in his work at the very beginning of his ministry. He still goes to the patriarchate to print *Al-Kiraza* magazine, just as he did as a young man. But there have also been many changes since that time. He can contact his prayer-partner at any moment by mobile phone. When he enters the patriarchate he must now put on the black bulbous hat befitting his rank as *Qomos* in the Coptic Church. But to Father Simaan, these changes matter not a jot. He is still essentially a priest in his parish.

It is not as if God were demanding more from him than from others. Perhaps, he reasons, his call is fulfilled and God is preparing those who will carry on. In the old days, particularly in Egypt, the vision was that the work was all down to one person. When that individual's contribution came to an end, so did the entire ministry. This, Father

Simaan feels strongly, is no way to work. If a key person – such as his spiritual guide, Father Zakariya Butros – were to leave or die, then that is not the end.

Father Simaan is only too well aware that he could very well pass away at any time, should this be God's will. To remind himself of this he keeps an empty coffin propped up against the wall by his desk! There is a coffin in his office at the church below the mountain and one at the retreat centre. They act as a stark reminder to the visitor that *now* is the time to reckon with God. The sight reminds those who rely on Father Simaan to keep the ministry going, that they have to depend on Jesus. If Father Simaan dies, will the work stop? 'Of course not!' is his devout hope.

The church is doing everything it can to ensure that there will be many generations that follow on. Young people educated at the church school have been trained to be leaders in the church and are now the main deacons, Sunday school teachers and youth leaders. This is truly an indigenous church.

Father Simaan recalls that the omnicompetent priests of old used to wander all over Egypt, but God said to Father Simaan, 'Don't move away from this place. This is your calling and your ministry. Here.' So Father Simaan doesn't go anywhere else in Egypt at all, because he knows that God wants him in Manshiyat Nasir.

Yet he has no problem at all with people coming *to him*. And that is what is happening – thousands of people come – but Father Simaan is still a local priest. He takes the view that if the Holy Spirit wants someone to come, he will bring them. All those God wants to come will come. There is no need for Father Simaan to go out and pull them in – this is not his work.

Nevertheless, if people are committed to coming regularly,

then the church helps to organize transport for them. Many groups come by bus to the Thursday meetings. They are willing to come into the rubbish tips and the bad smells because God is leading them. For a long time, one *zeballeen* group outside Manshiyat Nasir asked Father Simaan to come to them. He didn't go at first, then finally he agreed to lead a service for them once a month. 'They want it twice a month, but that is impossible,' he says.

If Father Simaan does travel outside Manshiyat Nasir – or outside the *zeballeen* areas – he does not do any preaching, because that is not his calling. Yet he would be willing to give a testimony at a conference outside Egypt, because overseas he would not be competing with anyone else's ministry. To take the opportunity to share what is happening at the mountain he sees simply as witnessing to the work of God.

Father Simaan's vision is that those who come in to the ministry on the mountain will then go out into the world. As the *zeballeen* turn to Christ they will be a cause of blessing to all Egypt. They can go down into the heart of Egypt to places he cannot go – or to places no one else can visit. They go into every house, flat and street. So people get to meet the *zeballeen* away from their usual surroundings. They don't just see in them their background and all the associations that has. What they see in them is Christ.

The Gold Watch

One American came to Father Simaan and told him that he turned to Christ because of an Egyptian rubbish collector in Garden City in Cairo. He'd lost a really expensive gold watch and one day found someone knocking on his door and saying to him,

'Haven't you lost something?'

He thought, 'It's someone wearing a *galibeyya* – why is he coming to me?'

'Yes – and I've asked everyone in every flat in the block,' the American said aloud.

'But is this what you've lost?' persisted the stranger. 'It looks like gold.' And he got it out of his pocket.

When he saw the watch the American invited his visitor into the flat. When they were sitting down he asked, 'Tell me, why didn't you keep it yourself?'

He replied, 'Christ taught me, give to Caesar what is Caesar's and to God what is God's' (Matthew 22.21).

'But why didn't you take it and wear it?' the American persisted.

'It's not mine – it's not my right. I must be honest – it's not my watch – Christ gave me life.'

The American said to him, 'Are you a Christian?'

'Yes,' the man replied.

The American then continued, 'I am an atheist, and I hated Christ. But because of you I will live for the Christ you live for.'

And, miraculously, this atheist was transformed into a Christian who is now a *khaadim* (church worker). He wrote in his diary, 'I came back to Christ from atheism because of an Egyptian Christian garbage collector in Garden City, Cairo.' This rubbish collector was called Yusuf.

These are the living signs of the practical Christian life, as Father Simaan sees them: not words but deeds. 'Let your light shine before men, that they may see your good deeds and praise your Father in heaven' (Matthew 5.16). Everyone should be light from Christ and salt for the earth. Many people hear the hymns the *zeballeen* sing when they come in the morning to collect the rubbish. Because of the *zebaal*, many come to the mountain, hear the voice of God, and come back to Christ.

Twenty-five years of ministry among the *zeballeen* has not changed Father Simaan's firm conviction that evangelism is not just a matter of proclaiming the word, but also of practical living. This principle applies to discipleship. He says, 'How can these believers live a life of ministry, of true discipleship to Christ in the church?' He answers his own question: 'As servants *really* living Christ.'

Some say that God's work is simply *kiraza* (witness with proclamation). Others do development projects. But Father Simaan certainly doesn't see his ministry as simply 'humanitarian'. All the work belongs to God and its goal is God's glory. The *kiraza* goes on through the gifts and experience of the lay-workers. In vacation periods, great numbers of them are committed to the work of evangelism.

The church takes in those who have made a beginning with God and lays on a meeting to build them up. They allow into that meeting, say, one hundred people. Then they make sure that each one of those one hundred has a priest to go to. This priest must give independent confirmation that his charge has really begun a spiritual life with God.

The church then divides the new believers into groups so that ministers who are already trained take ten of the new trainees. They lead meetings on topics like 'How to begin'; 'How to abide'; 'How to be built up'. After that they move on to 'Maturity'. Several stages go to make up each level, so that in every level no one gets less than three years' training. Father Simaan feels a lay-worker needs at least that length of time to be equipped to minister to others.

A group that starts with ten trainees can be cut down if

someone does not complete one stage of the course. The church is grateful to have hundreds of young women who are serving, including some married women. The same applies to young men – so they now have around 700 or 800 people who can serve, some of whom have had fifteen years' training.

This is first of all a call, a responsibility, and a trust. Father Simaan doesn't feel he has anything unusual to offer. The call he has is for evangelism and teaching, with the aim of saving the soul and building it up. If you asked him to change his method he couldn't, because this is the way the Lord has put his task into his hands. There are many churches that share the bread and wine at communion; they offer public prayers and sing psalms. In fact, they go through all the motions, but they don't do them *expecting* God to work through them.

Just to speak words knowing that the Holy Spirit can work through them, can be a great thing, says Father Simaan. The people who wrote those words down were saints. The saints did great deeds – and they were controlled by the Holy Spirit. But we can say or pray their words out loud without expecting the Holy Spirit to be in them, so they lose their force and effect, and it just ends up as a matter of ordinary routine. Getting involved in church life is all well and good, but we need to breathe the oxygen the Church lives by – we need to breathe the Spirit.

Father Simaan insists that the secret of his ministry is the Holy Spirit – not him. If he approaches ministry in an 'I'-centred way, and asks himself 'What shall I say to the people, and how should I speak?' then everything goes in one ear of the people and out the other! But when the Holy Spirit speaks, his words go to the heart.

Yet Father Simaan still sees himself as an ignoramus

when it comes to teaching. I asked him, 'How has your ministry among the *zeballeen* influenced your theology?'

'Theology?' he echoed, incredulous. 'I don't know anything about theology. I'm just a rubbish collector!'

He also readily admits that he makes a lot of mistakes. Sometimes he gets Bible verses wrong. But he trusts the Holy Spirit to put things right, because he is the one who is at work.

The Holy Spirit fills the one who submits completely and uses the person who has the vision to see that it is the Holy Spirit who does the work. Father Simaan prays, 'Lord, empty me, take the blockages out of me, wash me and purify me. Give me, O Lord, the filling for the work of the Holy Spirit, from the Holy Spirit.' He testifies that when he places himself in God's hands and understands the goal that is set before him, then the Lord lifts him up. God frees him from obstructive thoughts and emotional barriers.

When all the 'baggage' has been dealt with, he can make a fresh start before the Holy Spirit – set apart, emptied and ready. 'God begins to fill me. He gives me this fullness. And this fullness begins every day to be renewed and to increase.' The Holy Spirit, he points out, is present within us, not outside us. The important thing is that the Holy Spirit has his way within us.

If the Holy Spirit is within us yet we don't see him, then we have lost sight of the goal. But 'you yourselves are God's temple and . . . God's Spirit lives in you' (1 Corinthians 3.16). 'Do you not know that your body is a temple of the Holy Spirit, who is in you, whom you have received from God? You are not your own; you were bought at a price. Therefore honour God with your body' (1 Corinthians 6.19–20). If we know that the Holy Spirit is in us, but don't give him the jurisdiction to *work* in us, he won't work. But if we have understood that the Holy Spirit wants to work within us and we give him his freedom and power and authority, he will work.

Sometimes someone turns to Christ, plunges into activity and forgets to talk with Christ and enjoy him. The Spirit is then not free to work and this person's ministry will be ordinary, like any other ministry. But those who set their hearts on being renewed by the Holy Spirit within them must take time out with the Lord. From time to time they need to go on a retreat, to be with Jesus. Then the Holy Spirit can renew them and have more of them.

Having done this himself and experienced it, Father Simaan has a word of warning against complacency. If we imagine the day will come when we can say 'I am filled with the Holy Spirit' and that's the end of the story, that won't do. It's an ongoing thing. It's not a matter of *Kul As-Sena wa Enta Tayyib* (a greeting meaning 'every year you'll be fine'). In spiritual terms this is like saying, 'I'm all right, Jack.' Every day we must take new power, new fullness, and ask the Lord to make us overflow with the Holy Spirit. This is something that must continue throughout life.

The fact that outstanding spiritual experiences are not an end in themselves is amply borne out by the history of ministry on the mountain. Not everyone who experiences miracles turns to Christ. There are those who repent and those who don't, just as when Christ healed the ten lepers and only one came back to him (Luke 17.12–19).

Among the examples Father Simaan cites 'is one whom the Lord raised from the dead [see Chapter 6]. He had fallen from the mountain and his whole body was broken in pieces with a sound that was loud and clear. A doctor was there – we got him up from below – so when our Lord raised him the doctor was standing there to verify it.'

For five and a half years the ministry team tried to help this man to follow Christ, but he never committed himself and never came to a personal knowledge of God. 'He never knew our Lord. More important than being raised from the dead is that the person repents of his sin. He can be living, but still dead.'

What then was God doing through that miracle?

'The Lord . . . confirmed his word by the signs that accompanied it' (Mark 16.20 *NIV*). When between fifty and seventy believers see a man plunge to his death and pray for his healing, then witness God raising him to life, that builds up their faith. For they have prayed, and after they have prayed God raises him up. 'It's not we who raise up, it is Christ who raises up' avers Father Simaan. 'Those who turn to Christ find that he is the one who works.'

It would be hard to find a less man-centred vision of ministry. For Father Simaan, God is the God who acts.

NOTES

2 A Mountain to Move

1. See A'bd Al Fatah, N., and Rashwaan, D. (eds), 'The Rubbish Collectors' Community', pp. 265–9.
2. Ibrahim, Qomos S., *The Pope Loves Them*, pp. 22–3.
3. See note 2, pp. 30–1.
4. Yohanna, Pastor M., 'The History of the Coptic Church'. Quoted in Anon., *The Biography of St Samaan*, p. 15.
5. Al-Masri, I., 'The Story of the Coptic Church', part 3. Quoted in Anon., *The Biography of St Samaan*, p. 15.
6. Anba Isodorus, 'Al-Khareeda Al-Nafeesa fi Tareekh Al-Kaneesa'. Quoted in Anon., *The Biography of St Samaan*, pp. 18–19.
7. Al-Masri, I., 'The Story of the Coptic Church', part 3. Quoted in Anon., *The Biography of St Samaan*, p. 20.
8. See note 7.

3 Earthquake

1. cf. 1 Corinthians 10.13.

4 The Voice

1. See Musk, W., *The Unseen Face of Islam*, p. 16.

5 Stones or Souls?

1. Anon., *The Biography of St Samaan*, pp. 71–2.

2. See A'bd Al-Fatah, N., and Rashwaan, D. (eds), 'The Rubbish Collectors' Community', pp. 265–9.
3. See Ibrahim, Qomos S., *The Pope Loves Them*, pp. 21–2.
4. Jenkins, S., 'Faith to Move Mountains', p. 13.
5. For a full account of the French campaign, see Moorehead, A., *The Blue Nile*, Part 2.
6. See Ward, B., *The Wisdom of the Desert Fathers*, p. ix.
7. See note 4.
8. See note 4.

6 Miracles

1. See 'How the Body of St Samaan the Tanner was Discovered' in Anon., *The Biography of St Samaan*, pp. 95–102 (esp. p. 96).
2. Source: magazine programme *Jan En Alleman*, EO Television, Holland, 1995.
3. See note 2.
4. Houston, T., 'No Little People'.
5. Ibrahim, Qomos S., *The Pope Loves Them*, p. 39.
6. Parry, E. G., *Some Ancient and Younger Churches*, p. 6.
7. See Jenkins, S., 'Faith to Move Mountains', p. 12.

7 Service

1. Comment made by team member.

8 Healing

1. Dr Adly F. Ghaly, an Associate Member of the Royal College of Pathologists, diagnosed 'Ewing's Sarcoma of the Upper Tibia' in a report dated 17 June 1991. In a slide consultation on 19 June 1991, Dr Saad S. Eissa, Professor of Pathology at the National Cancer Institute of Cairo University, found 'sheets of closely packed malignant small rounded cells'. The tumour had 'infiltrated the bone and bone marrow'.
2. McConchie, B., *The Renewal of the Garbage Collectors*, quoted in a letter to Father Simaan dated 15 May 1996.

9 New Hearts

1. Sara was probably monitored with a continuous electro-cardiogram, after making her main blood vessels radio opaque. Blood vessels can also be monitored through an angiogram or an angio-cardiogram.
2. This testimony was given by Sara at a meeting at the Muqattam 'monastery' on 14 August 1996. In accordance with the rules for such meetings, she mentioned neither Father Simaan nor the retreat centre by name. The reason for this rule was to give the glory to God.

FURTHER READING

A'bd Al-Fatah, N., and Rashwaan, D. (eds), 'The Rubbish Collectors' Community at Manshiyat Nasir: A Study of the State of the Relationship Between The Religious Foundation and the Local Social Reality', in *Al-Halat Al-Diniyah fi Misr – The State of Religion in Egypt* (Cairo, Al-Ahram, 1995).

Anon., *The Biography of St Samaan the Shoemaker 'the Tanner'* (Cairo, The Church of St Simaan the Tanner, 1983). First English edn 1994.

Assad, M., 'Mission in the Coptic Orthodox Church', *International Review of Mission*, vol. 80, 1991.

Hourani, A., *A History of the Arab Peoples* (Faber, 1991).

Houston, T., 'No Little People', Lausanne Committee for World Evangelization, *World Evangelization*, December 1996–January 1997.

Ibrahim, Qomos S., *Ha'ula Ahibhum Il Baba – The Pope Loves Them* (Cairo, Priests of the Church of St Simaan the Tanner, 1996).

Jenkins, S., 'Faith to Move Mountains', *Cairo Times*, 20 March–2 April 1997.

McConchie, B., *The Renewal of the Garbage Collectors* (World Vision International, 1996).

Moorehead, A., *The Blue Nile* (Penguin, 1983).

Musk, W., *The Unseen Face of Islam* (MARC, 1989).

Parry, E. G., *Some Ancient and Younger Churches in Egypt* (Cairo, SPCK, 1942).

Ward, B., *The Wisdom of the Desert Fathers* (Oxford, SLG Press, 1986).